Information Security Incident and Data Breach Management

A Step-by-Step Approach

John Kyriazoglou

Apress®

Information Security Incident and Data Breach Management:
A Step-by-Step Approach

John Kyriazoglou
Toronto, ON, Canada

ISBN-13 (pbk): 979-8-8688-0869-2   ISBN-13 (electronic): 979-8-8688-0870-8
https://doi.org/10.1007/979-8-8688-0870-8

Managing Director, Apress Media LLC: Welmoed Spahr
Acquisitions Editor: Susan McDermott
Development Editor: Laura Berendson
Project Manager: Jessica Vakili

Cover image from Pixabay

Distributed to the book trade worldwide by Springer Science+Business Media New York, 1 New York Plaza, Suite 4600, New York, NY 10004-1562, USA. Phone 1-800-SPRINGER, fax (201) 348-4505, e-mail orders-ny@springer-sbm.com, or visit www.springeronline.com. Apress Media, LLC is a California LLC and the sole member (owner) is Springer Science + Business Media Finance Inc (SSBM Finance Inc). SSBM Finance Inc is a **Delaware** corporation.

For information on translations, please e-mail booktranslations@springernature.com; for reprint, paperback, or audio rights, please e-mail bookpermissions@springernature.com.

Apress titles may be purchased in bulk for academic, corporate, or promotional use. eBook versions and licenses are also available for most titles. For more information, reference our Print and eBook Bulk Sales web page at http://www.apress.com/bulk-sales.

Any source code or other supplementary material referenced by the author in this book is available to readers on GitHub. For more detailed information, please visit https://www.apress.com/gp/services/source-code.

If disposing of this product, please recycle the paper

This book is dedicated to my family – Sandy, Miranda, Chris, Dimitri, and Melina, our most precious gem on this planet.

Table of Contents

About the Author

John Kyriazoglou is a Certified Internal Controls Auditor (CICA) and obtained a BA (Honors) from the University of Toronto, Canada, also having earned a scholastic award for Academic Excellence in Computer Science. John has worked in Canada, England, Switzerland, Luxembourg, Greece, Saudi Arabia, and other countries for over 40 years as a senior IT manager, managing director of an IT Services Company, and as an IT and data privacy auditor and consultant, with a variety of clients and projects, in both the private and the public sector (jkyriazoglou@hotmail.com).

John is also currently the editor in chief of *TheIIC Internal Controls e-Magazine* and represents Western Europe on the Advisory Board of the Institute for Internal Controls. He is also consulting on data privacy and IT security issues (GDPR, e-privacy, etc.) to a large number of private and public clients and has published several books on these issues.

John is the creator of

1. The DP&P system (data protection and privacy system)

2. The PANDORA WAY (approach and practices to improve your business and personal life)

3. The OCCUP approach (strategies for reducing occupational stress)

4. The seven-milestones approach (setting goals for improving your personal and family life)

5. Various management tools (for privacy, IT auditing, data protection compliance, etc.)

John has also written numerous articles and several books (over 100) on data privacy, business management controls, IT strategic and operational controls, teleworking (remote working), and ancient Greek wisdom. For a full list of John's books, see https://bookboon.com/en/author/0908031c-ce02-9b86-11e6-6dd97b3999d1.

About the Technical Reviewer

 **Priyanka Neelakrishnan** is a distinguished product leader in the field of cybersecurity, bringing over a decade of demonstrated expertise in crafting premier security solutions. Her career is marked by influential roles at the world's leading cybersecurity firms, where she has conceptualized, strategized, developed, and launched innovative data security products tailored for enterprises of all sizes.

Under her leadership, Priyanka has managed a cybersecurity product portfolio valued at over $250 million, resulting in significant industry advancements and widespread adoption of her solutions. She is renowned for developing the first cloud enterprise data security solution utilizing award-winning content detection technologies for large enterprises. As a pioneer in leveraging AI, her projects include advanced data classifiers, supervised and unsupervised learning methodologies, and user behavior analytics, all contributing to autonomous data security solutions. Her groundbreaking work has earned her many accolades in the information security field.

As a recognized authority in data protection, Priyanka is also a published author and a technical reviewer for security books and journals. She is an independent researcher and a celebrated speaker at major conferences, contributing her insights and knowledge to advance the field of cybersecurity.

Acknowledgments

I wish to thank and acknowledge the excellent support provided to me by all Apress staff during the publishing process of this book: Susan McDermott, Sowmya Thodur, Jessica Vakili, Joseph Quatela.

Also, I wish to express my sincere gratitude to my clients that I have supported during my long career on various IT and privacy issues who have provided me with the necessary practical experience to make this book a real tool for all to consider for managing information security and data breaches as effectively as possible.

I also wish to thank the reviewer of this book, Priyanka Neelakrishnan, for her excellent and practical comments.

Prologue: Information Security Incident and Data Breach Management Approach

Introduction

Information security incidents and data breaches can quickly escalate into business crises, leading to financial loss, legal consequences, compliance fines and sanctions, service disruption, and damage to reputation and customer trust.

A set of well-managed measures for managing information incidents and data breaches is a key component of an information security program. Such response plans or procedures help mitigate the impact of an attack, remediate vulnerabilities, and secure your overall organization in a coordinated manner. It also ensures that your organization can utilize manpower, tools, and resources to efficiently tackle the issue and minimize its impact on other operations.

Also, effective data breach response is about reducing or removing harm to affected individuals, while protecting the interests of your organization or company.

Breaches of personal data can result in significant harm, including people having their identities stolen or the private home addresses of protected or vulnerable people being disclosed.

Incidents and data breaches can have a huge impact on an organization in terms of cost, fines and sanctions, productivity, and reputation. However, good incident and data breach management will reduce the impact when they do happen. Being able to detect and quickly respond to incidents and data breaches will help to prevent further damage, reducing the financial and operational impact.

It is therefore critical for all managers and leaders of organizations to develop and implement measures to respond to information security incidents and data breaches effectively.

Information Security Incident and Data Breach Response Approach

On the basis of my varied IT and auditing consulting experience, I recommend the following four-phase, seven-milestones approach to support and assist you in achieving these information security incident and data breach objectives.

Phase A	**Security and Breach Obligations and Requirements Comprehension**
Phase B	**Security and Privacy Framework Assurance**
Phase C	**Security Incident and Data Breach Response Management**
Phase D	**Security and Breach Response Process Evaluation**

Phase A: Security and Breach Obligations and Requirements Comprehension

Milestone 1: Understand information security and breach obligations.

    Action 1: Review the security obligations of ISO 27001 (the International Information Security Standard).

    Action 2: Ensure you understand the data breach notification obligations of your relevant privacy regulation affecting your operations.

    Action 3: Review and ensure you understand what are information security incidents and data breaches.

    See Chapter 1 for more details.

Milestone 2: Understand ISO 27K and privacy requirements.

    Action 1: Review and ensure you understand the control requirements of ISO 27001.

    Action 2: Review and ensure you understand the aspects of major privacy regulations (e.g., GDPR and LGPD).

    See Chapter 2 for more details.

Phase B: Security and Privacy Framework Assurance

Milestone 3: Ensure effective IT governance and privacy controls.

    Step 1: Define security roles and responsibilities

    Step 2: Ensure effective implementation of IT policies

    Step 3: Ensure staff are trained on security

    Step 4: Prepare for data breach management

    Step 5: Train employees on data privacy

    Step 6: Understand data flows

    Step 7: Review measures, technology, and third parties

    See Chapter 3 for more details.

Phase C: Security Incident and Data Breach Response Management

Milestone 4: Manage security incident responses.

   Step 1: Discover security incidents

   Step 2: Communicate security incidents

   Step 3: Analyze and evaluate security incidents

   Step 4: Determine response strategy to security incidents

   Step 5: Contain damage due to security incidents

   Step 6: Prevent reinfection

   Step 7: Restore affected systems

   Step 8: Document the incident

   Step 9: Report the incident

   Step 10: Preserve evidence

   See Chapter 4 for more details.

Milestone 5: Investigate cybercrimes

Step 1: Conduct initial assessment

Step 2: Confirm investigator readiness

Step 3: Ensure evidence collection

Step 4: Conduct incident analysis

Step 5: Craft and issue report

Step 6: Review findings and issues

Step 7: Improve methodology

See Chapter 5 for more details.

Milestone 6: Manage data breach responses.

Step 1: Ensure data breach management readiness

Step 2: Identify data breaches

Step 3: Investigate data breaches

Step 4: Respond to data breaches

Step 5: Preserve evidence

Step 6: Notify authorities and individuals

Step 7: Maintain data breach documentation

See Chapter 6 for more details.

Phase D: Security and Breach Response Process Evaluation

Milestone 7: Improve information incident and breach response process.

Step 1: Assess information governance controls framework

Step 2: Assess security incident cost

Step 3: Review information incident response process and measures

Step 4: Assess data breach management process and measures

Step 5: Review lessons learned

Step 6: Improve processes and measures

See Chapter 7 for more details.

Security Incident and Breach Response Objectives

The objectives of incident and breach response management are

1. The assurance that a security event or data breach has actually occurred

2. The maintenance or restoration of business continuity

3. Reducing the impact of the security incident or breach

4. Determining how the attack was made

5. The prevention of future attacks or incidents or breaches

6. Improving security incident response and data breach management

7. The prosecution of illegal activity

8. Informing the management about the situation and the response

Benefits of Incident Response and Data Breach Management

Managing information security incidents and data breaches is very critical for any private company or public organization to continue operations in the event of an emergency, especially in the case of a cybersecurity attack.

Some of the main advantages of following effective policies and procedures to manage information incidents and data breaches include various benefits. An incident response procedure will significantly reduce downtime for your company and will prove to the public that you are capable to face emergencies effectively and resume operations as best as possible.

Remaining in compliance is critical for many organizations, especially in the healthcare and legal industries. Failure to follow data security protocols can result in substantial fines and costly lawsuits.

Many businesses cannot afford to take any shortcuts and violate these strict regulations. However, the creation of a business continuity plan and incident and data breach handling will help ensure that your organization follows all of the rules in your particular industry.

Audience

The audience of this book includes, as an example:

1. ISO 27001 implementation and transition project managers

2. ISO 27001 auditors and inspectors

3. Auditors (IT, internal, external, etc.)

4. IT managers and development staff

5. Senior executives, CISOs, and corporate security managers

6. Administration, HR managers, and staff

7. Compliance and data protection officers

8. Cybersecurity professionals

9. IT development, auditing, and security university students

10. Anyone else interested in information security issues

This book is a sequel to my other data protection and IT books.

I am totally responsible for any potential errors, omissions, and faults found in this book. Your comments are welcome and will be acknowledged. Also, contact me if you need any support or advice on any issue contained in this book.

The following chapters deal with incident response and data breach management.

CHAPTER 1

Information Security and Breach Definitions and Obligations

This chapter supports you to achieve your first milestone (Understand Information Security and Breach Obligations) of Phase A (Obligations and Requirements Comprehension). It describes several critical information security and breach-related terms, what are security incidents and data breaches, the security obligations of ISO 27001 (the International Information Security Standard) and of major privacy regulations, and the data breach notification obligations of companies according to privacy regulations (e.g., GDPR).

Definitions of Information Security and Breach-Related Terms

Security and data breach terms can be very complex and quite technical. Clear security and breach definitions help ensure everyone understands the concepts, reducing confusion and miscommunication.

Clear definitions are also essential for educating and training individuals in security and breach management practices. It is therefore very crucial to define various relevant and critical information security and data breach terms related to security incident and breach management, such as information security, threat actors, advanced persistent threat, malware, phishing, denial-of-service attack, ransomware, unauthorized access, attempted access, information security incident, controllers, processors, personal data, data subjects, and data breaches.

These are described next.

Definitions of Information Security and Threat Actors

Information Security

Information security (InfoSec) is the protection of important information against unauthorized access, disclosure, use, alteration, or disruption. It helps ensure that sensitive organizational data is available to authorized users, remains confidential, and maintains its integrity.[1]

Threat Actors

Threat actors, also known as cyberthreat actors or malicious actors, are individuals or groups that intentionally cause harm to digital devices or systems. Threat actors exploit vulnerabilities in computer systems, networks, and software to perpetuate various cyberattacks, including phishing, ransomware, and malware attacks. Examples are cybercriminals, nation-states, terrorist groups, thrill-seekers; insider threats, and hackers.[2]

Definitions of Various Critical Information Security Terms

Examples of common critical information security terms include advanced persistent threat, malware, phishing, denial-of-service attack, ransomware, unauthorized access, and attempted access.[3]

Advanced Persistent Threat

An advanced persistent threat is a cyberattack where criminals work together to steal data or infiltrate systems that often go undetected over an extended period of time. In most cases, these attacks are performed by nation-states seeking to undermine another government.

Malware

Malware is a type of malicious software that is designed to damage or disable computers. Malware can be used to steal data, take control of systems, or launch attacks on other computers.

There are many different types of malicious software, such as viruses, worms, Trojans, and ransomware. Malware can be spread through email attachments, infected websites, or compromised software.

Phishing

Phishing is a type of cyberattack that uses emails or websites that appear to be from legitimate sources in order to trick users into disclosing sensitive information or clicking on malicious links.

Denial-of-Service Attack

A denial-of-service attack (DoS attack) is a type of cyberattack that attempts to make a system or network unavailable to users. DoS attacks target websites or online services and can be used to take down entire systems. DoS attacks are usually carried out by flooding the target with traffic or requests until it can no longer handle the load and becomes unavailable. They can also be used to disable systems or networks by corrupting data, taking advantage of vulnerabilities, or overloading resources.

Ransomware

Ransomware is a type of malware that encrypts files or locks systems, making them inaccessible to users. It can be spread through email attachments, infected websites, or compromised software. This type of malware blocks access or encrypts assets, often forcing the user to pay a ransom to regain access to their device, files, or system.

Unauthorized Access

"Unauthorized access" refers to a person who gains logical or physical access without permission to a company's network, system, application, data, information, or other resources.

Attempted Access

"Attempted access" includes any activity aimed at accessing or identifying an information resource of the company (computer, network, network port, protocol, communication service, or any combination, etc.) for future illegal exploitation.

For more definitions, you may see my *IT Glossary* book in the "Additional Resources" section.

Definition of an Information Security Incident

An information security incident, according to NIST[4], is "an occurrence that actually or potentially jeopardizes the confidentiality, integrity, or availability of an information system or the information the system processes, stores, or transmits or that constitutes a violation or imminent threat of violation of security policies, security procedures, or acceptable use policies."

An information security incident is any one or more of the following:

1. Loss of confidential information (data theft)

2. Compromise of information integrity (data damage or unauthorized modification)

3. Theft of IT goods (software) and physical resources, including computers, storage devices, printers, etc.

4. Damage to physical IT assets including computers, storage and network devices, printers, etc.

5. Denial of service

6. Misuse of services, information, or assets

7. Contamination of systems by unauthorized or hostile software

8. An attempt of unauthorized access

9. Unauthorized changes to equipment, software, or configuration data

10. Reports of unusual system behavior

11. Responses to intrusion detection alarms

12. A violation of company computer security policies and standards

13. A virus

14. An unexpected or unusual program

15. A denial-of-service attack against a network, computers, or data

16. Misuse of service, systems, or information

17. Physical or logical damage to systems

18. Ransomware on multiple IT resources

19. Webserver or file server compromises that involve malware insertion or unauthorized access that goes undetected for a period of time

20. Database compromises that involve any unauthorized access that is undetected for a period of time

21. Any incident involving designated critical IT infrastructure

22. Loss or theft of any IT resource

23. A violation of any IT policies, standard, or code of conduct that threatens the confidentiality, integrity, or availability of corporate information

24. Insider threats (employees abusing their access rights to information, etc.)

25. IT sabotage

26. Security misconfigurations (security misconfigurations can range from out-of-date infrastructure to unchanged defaults, to missing values for security parameters, etc.).

Definitions of Controllers and Processors

The definitions according to GDPR of controllers and processors are as follows.

Controller

Controller means the natural or legal person, public authority, agency, or other body which, alone or jointly with others, determines the purposes and means of the processing of personal data; where the purposes and means of such processing are determined by Union or Member State law, the controller or the specific criteria for its nomination may be provided for by Union or Member State law.

Processor

Processor means a natural or legal person, public authority, agency, or other body which processes personal data on behalf of the controller.

Definition of Personal Data and Data Subjects

Personal Data

Personal data, as per GDPR Article 4, means "any information relating to an identified or identifiable natural person ('data subject')."

The following personal data, as per Articles 4, 9, 14, and 15 and Recitals 51 to 56, are considered "sensitive" and are subject to specific processing conditions: personal data revealing racial or ethnic origin, political opinions, religious, or philosophical beliefs; trade-union membership;

genetic data and biometric data processed solely to identify a human being; health-related data; and data concerning a person's sex life or sexual orientation.

Data Subject

Data subject, as per GDPR Article 4, means "an identifiable natural person is one who can be identified, directly or indirectly, in particular by reference to an identifier such as a name, an identification number, location data, an online identifier or to one or more factors specific to the physical, physiological, genetic, mental, economic, cultural or social identity of that natural person."

Definition of Data Breaches

A data breach, according to NIST[5], is "the loss of control, compromise, unauthorized disclosure, unauthorized acquisition, or any similar occurrence where: a person other than an authorized user accesses or potentially accesses personally identifiable information; or an authorized user accesses personally identifiable information for another than authorized purpose."

A data breach occurs when the data for which your company/organization is responsible suffers a security incident resulting in a breach of confidentiality, availability, or integrity[6].

A personal data breach is usually defined as "a breach of security leading to the accidental or unlawful destruction, loss, alteration, unauthorized disclosure of, or access to, personal data transmitted, stored, or otherwise processed in connection with the provision of a public electronic communications service."

A personal data breach may mean that someone other than the data controller gets unauthorized access to personal data. But a personal data breach can also occur if there is unauthorized access within an organization, or if a data controller's own employee accidentally or by malice or to gain some benefit, etc., alters or deletes or shares personal data.

In contrast to the typical security incident response, which concerns a broader range of incidents affecting information security, this control uses the term personal data breach incident to describe only those incidents that relate to personal data.

Examples (EX) of data breaches are outlined next.

EX01: An employee disclosed personal data to an external party without approval.

EX02: An external invader (hacker) accessed personal data of several data subjects and published them on the Internet.

EX03: Theft or loss of computers and laptops, portable electronic devices, electronic media, and paper files containing personal data without encryption or pseudonymization controls.

EX04: An employee received an email and clicked on a link to download a document that contained a virus. This virus infested several company systems that also contained sensitive data.

EX05: A backup tape with unencrypted personal data was lost on the way to being stored in a secure location.

EX06: A bank employee emailed a new client's file in error to a colleague in a different department who was not authorized to see any client information.

EX07: A bank employee posted a bank account statement to the wrong person.

EX08: An employee lost his briefcase, which contained his laptop with unencrypted personal data and various paper files with corporate financial data.

EX09: A controller maintains data in an online (cloud) service. As a result of a cyberattack on that service, personal data of individuals are stolen.

EX10: A direct marketing email is sent to a large number of recipients with all their email account names being visible to all recipients.

EX11: A controller suffers a ransomware attack which results in all data being encrypted.

EX12: A controller stored a backup of personal data encrypted on a USB key. The key is stolen during a break-in.

Security Obligations

Security plays a primary role in the ISO 27001 Information Security Standard (see Chapter 2) and most major privacy and data protection regulatory regimes (e.g., EU's GDPR, Brazil's LGPD, Canada's PIPEDA, China's Personal Information Protection Law (PIPL), etc. See Chapter 2 for a summary of highlights of ISO 27K, GDPR, and LGPD). The principle of transparency in all privacy regulations allows individuals to exercise their rights and get assurance by organizations that their personal data are always secure. For example, appropriate mechanisms for international data transfers or other types of personal data processing by processors are of little value to individuals if their data are not secure. A lack of consumer trust has been identified as a key risk to the development of the digital single market, and a number of high-profile data breaches have exacerbated the situation. Therefore, all privacy regulations have made data security a critical part of everyday life.

Security obligations apply to both controllers (companies holding personal data) and processors (companies processing personal data). This makes sense in today's world, where service providers can have a large influence on the security measures taken and have already established complex subcontracting agreements that they may find impractical or undesirable to seek to modify. With rules directly applicable to both controllers and processors offering goods or services all over the world, any company that processes personal data must have an idea of the security obligations that apply to it.

Both controllers and processors are obliged to "apply appropriate technical and organizational measures" taking into account "the development of technology and implementation costs" and "the nature, scope, context and purpose of the processing and the risk or varying probability and severity to the rights and freedoms of natural persons."

In addition, privacy regulations require controllers to only engage processors that provide "adequate guarantees for the implementation of appropriate technical and organizational measures" in order to meet the requirements of the relevant data protection or privacy regime and protect the rights of individuals (data subjects).

The following are specific guidelines for the types of security actions that may be considered appropriate for the risk. These guidelines include

- The ability to ensure the continued confidentiality, integrity, availability, and resilience of processing systems and services

- The ability to promptly restore availability and access to personal data in the event of a physical or technical event, such as a data breach

- Pseudonymization and encryption of personal data

- A process of regularly testing and evaluating the effectiveness of technical and organizational measures to ensure the security of processing

The above guidelines show that "security" is not only about external threats but also covers issues of continued operation.

The steps that will support your efforts to manage information security incidents in the best way possible are included in Chapters 4 and 5.

Data Breach Notification Obligations

A data breach occurs when the personal data for which your company or organization responsible suffers a security incident resulting in a breach of confidentiality, availability, or integrity. If that occurs, and it is likely that the breach poses a risk to an individual's rights and freedoms, your company or organization has to notify the supervisory authority and the persons concerned.

All privacy regulations include specific breach notification guidelines. According to these, so-called "personal data breaches" should be notified, by the controllers to the supervisory authorities and in some cases also to the affected individuals.

Failure to comply with GDPR to protect personal data can result in potentially hefty **fines** — namely, up to 4% of a company's annual global revenues or 20 million euros ($22.8 million), whichever is the bigger amount.

Therefore, it is vital for your company or organization to implement appropriate technical and organizational measures to avoid possible information security incidents and data breaches.

The steps that will support your efforts to manage data breaches in the best way possible are included in Chapter 6.

Recommended Actions

The following actions are recommended to help you understand better what are incidents and data breaches as well as the information security incident and data breach obligations of your company or organization.

These are

Action 1: Review and understand the critical information security and data breach terms related to security incident and breach management described above), such as information security, threat actors, advanced persistent threat, malware, phishing, denial-of-service attack, ransomware, unauthorized access, attempted access, information security incident, controllers, processors, personal data, data subjects, and data breaches.

Action 2: Review and ensure you understand what are information security incidents and data breaches.

Action 3: Review the security obligations of ISO 27001 (the International Information Security Standard). For more details, you may also access my ISO books in "Additional Resources" section.

Action 4: Ensure you understand the data breach notification obligations of your company according to your relevant privacy regulation affecting your operations. For more details on privacy regulations, like GDPR, you may also access my data protection books in the "Additional Resources" section.

Action 5: In addition to the previous actions, you may want to review and ensure you understand the following OECD Digital Security Principles (DSP[7]):

> **DSP1:** Digital security culture: awareness, skills, and empowerment
>
> **DSP2:** Responsibility and liability
>
> **DSP3:** Human rights and fundamental values
>
> **DSP4:** Cooperation
>
> **DSP5:** Strategy and governance
>
> **DSP6:** Risk assessment and treatment cycle
>
> **DSP7:** Security measures
>
> **DSP8:** Innovation
>
> **DSP9:** Resilience, preparedness, and continuity

Conclusion

Understanding the information security incident and data breach obligations and what are incidents and data breaches helps you prepare better in order to achieve your next milestone (Milestone 2) more effectively. Executing the five recommended actions completes the achievement of the first part of Milestone 1 (Understand Information Security and Breach Obligations) of Phase A (Obligations and Requirements Comprehension).

CHAPTER 2

Summarizing ISO 27K and Major Privacy Regulations

This chapter supports you to achieve your second milestone (Understand ISO 27K and Privacy Requirements) of Phase A (Obligations and Requirements Comprehension). It contains a summary of highlights of ISO 27001 Information Security Standard and the two major privacy regulations for European Union (GDPR) and Brazil (LGPD).

ISO 27001 Summary

ISO/IEC 27001 is the world's best-known standard for **information security management systems (ISMS)**. It defines requirements an ISMS must meet.

The ISO/IEC 27001 standard provides companies of any size and from all sectors of activity with guidance for establishing, implementing, maintaining, and continually improving an information security management system.

Conformity with ISO/IEC 27001 means that an organization or business has put in place a system to manage risks related to the security of data owned or handled by the company and that this system respects all the best practices and principles enshrined in this international standard[1].

An information security management system (**ISMS**) is the structured management of information deemed sensitive and the risks that threaten it, in order to keep it secure.

ISO/IEC 27001 is an international standard that specifies the requirements that an organization must meet in order to comprehensively and effectively manage its information security.

The ISO 27001 standard is at an organizational level intertwined with the concept of information security and contains the requirements for the creation, implementation, and improvement of an information security management system.

It is a set of corporate information security measures (plans, policies, procedures, etc.) aimed at protecting corporate data from the most possible and serious risks, in order to minimize the chances of their loss, leakage, harm, or other damage so that the inability of serving corporate customers and other interested parties is minimized if not avoided all-together.

These corporate security measures concern the protection of the corporate information at the following four levels, such as organizational, people, physical, and technological.

Examples of the information security measures are information security policy, information security roles and responsibilities, personnel screening, physical security controls, back-up and recovery procedures, firewalls, encrypting information and data, personal data protection controls, etc.

New Version of ISO 27001

ISO 27001:2022 replaces 27001:2013 being the new international standard issued for information security by the International Organization for Standardization (ISO). The new title of the 27001:2022 standard is Information security, cybersecurity, and privacy protection – Information security management systems – Requirements, in contrast to 27001:2013 which is Information technology – Security techniques – Information security management systems – Requirements.

As in all transitions to new editions of standards, a three-year transitional period is provided for adapting to the requirements of the new standard from the date of its publication, with a final date of October 31, 2025.

At the same time, the International Organization for Standardization (ISO) has published the revised version of ISO27002, which is an integral part (Annex A) of ISO27001.

Information security was, is, and will be one of the most serious issues for a modern business, and the ISO 27001 standard is one of the most reliable ways to ensure it[1].

GDPR Summary

The European General Data Protection Regulation (GDPR for short[2]) is built around two key principles: giving data subjects (customers, passengers, employees, crew members, patients, citizens, etc.) more control of their personal data and simplifying regulations for international businesses with a unifying regulation that stands across the European Union (EU).

GDPR Highlights

The major highlights of this regulation relate to the following criteria:

1. Personal Data Definitions

1. The GDPR applies to all personal data that is collected in the EU, regardless of where in the world it is processed. Any database containing personal or sensitive data collected within the EU will be in scope, as will any media containing personal or sensitive data. Any organization that has such data in its systems, regardless of business size or sector, will have to comply with the GDPR.

2. Personal data is anything that can identify a "natural person" ("data subject") and can include information such as a name, a photo, an email address (including work email address), bank details, posts on social networking websites, medical information or even an IP address, etc.

3. "Sensitive personal data" are personal data, revealing racial or ethnic origin, political opinions, religious or philosophical beliefs, trade-union membership; data concerning health or sex life and sexual orientation; and genetic data or biometric data.

2. Data Protection Principles

Organizations must ensure that all processing operations of personal data must adhere to and comply with the following principles: "Lawfulness, fairness and transparency," "Purpose limitation," "Data minimization,"

"Accuracy," "Storage limitation," "Integrity and confidentiality," and "Accountability."

To satisfy the requirements of these principles, every personal data controller and processor must implement appropriate risk-based technical and organizational measures and procedures to ensure compliance with GDPR.

3. PD Collection, Consent, and Legal Basis

A data controller or processor is not allowed to collect more personal data than needed for the processing and must specify the legal basis for all personal data processing.

When the legal basis demands a consent from the data subject prior to processing, this (consent) must be obtained in accordance with GDPR. Consent to process data must be freely given and for specific purposes by data subjects.

Data subjects must be informed of their right to withdraw their consent. Consent must be explicit in the case of sensitive personal data or transborder dataflows.

4. Informing Data Subjects

The controller is obligated to inform (via a privacy notice) the data subjects about the processing of their personal data when it comes to how, when, and where it is processed, the legal basis, security measures and the subject's rights, etc.

5. Satisfying the Rights of Data Subjects

There are several rights, such as

1. The right to be forgotten, i.e., the right to ask data controllers to erase all personal data without undue delay in certain circumstances

2. The right to data portability, i.e., the right of individuals that have provided personal data to a service provider, to require the provider to transfer or "port" the data to another service provider provided this is feasible

3. The right to object to profiling, i.e., the right not to be subject to a decision based solely on automated processing, etc.

The controller is obligated to satisfy these rights in a proper way.

6. Data Protection Officer (DPO)

Some organizations must appoint a DPO regardless of their size, services and products offered, and number of employees, customers, etc. Companies whose activities involve "regular or systematic" monitoring of data subjects on a large scale (in other words processing extensive personal information), or which involve processing large volumes of "special category data," must employ a data protection officer (DPO).

7. Controllers and Processors

The GDPR applies to both "controllers" and "processors."

A controller is the entity that decides the purpose of the data processing activities. For example, if you're a small business offering a plumbing service and your customer details are managed using a customer information system hosted by a third party, this would generally make you the controller and the third party the processor.

8. Mandatory Breach Notification

1. Organizations must notify supervisory authority of data breaches "without undue delay" or within 72 hours, unless the breach is unlikely to be a risk to individuals.

2. If there is a high risk to data subjects, then such data subjects should also be informed.

For more details, also see my GDPR and data protection and privacy books in the "Additional Resources" section.

LGPD Highlights

LGPD[3] is the first comprehensive general data protection law in Latin America. Besides the LGPD, other sectoral laws and statutes in Brazil also address privacy and data protection rights and, in many cases, support and complement the privacy requirements of LGPD.

These include The Civil Code, The Internet Act, The Consumer Protection Code, The Wiretap Act, etc.

Law 13.709 of Brazil is the general law for the protection of personal data or, in Portuguese, the Lei Geral de Proteção de Dados Pessoais ("LGPD") and was sanctioned by the former president of Brazil, Michel Temer, in August of 2018.

The LGPD applies to all personal data that is collected in Brazil, regardless of where in the world it is processed. Any database containing personal or sensitive data collected within Brazil will be in scope, as will any media containing personal or sensitive data. Any organization that has such data in its systems, regardless of business size or sector, will have to comply with the LGPD.

The major highlights of this law, in summary, are outlined next.

Data Protection Principles

Organizations must ensure that all processing operations of personal data must adhere to and comply with the following principles (LGPD Article 6):

Principle 1. Purpose: You must ensure that you carry out the processing of personal data for legitimate, specific, and explicit purposes of which the data subject (holder) is informed, with no possibility of subsequent processing that is incompatible with these purposes.

Principle 2. Adequacy: You must ensure that there is compatibility of the processing of personal data with the purposes communicated to the data subject (holder), in accordance with the context of the processing.

Principle 3. Necessity: You must only process personal data that is necessary for the fulfilment of your stated purposes of processing.

Principle 4. Free Access: Data subjects (holders) must be able to freely exercise their rights under the law and have unencumbered, easy access to any information about the processing of their personal data, without any charge.

Principle 5. Quality of the Data: You, the controller, must ensure the data subjects of integrity and accuracy of the personal data processed and keep it updated and relevant, in accordance with the purpose for processing such personal data.

Principle 6. Transparency: Information about your processing of personal data must be clear, accurate and easily available to data subjects (holders). Data subjects must also be able to access information about the third parties that you, the controller, share their personal data with.

Principle 7. Security: Both the controller and any processors must be sure to implement technical and administrative measures in order to protect personal data from unauthorized access, accidental or unlawful destruction, loss, alteration and unauthorized communication, or dissemination.

Principle 8. Prevention: It's the responsibility of both the controller and the processor to adopt technical and organizational measures to prevent any damage being caused by the processing of personal data.

Principle 9. Nondiscrimination: No processing of personal data should occur for discriminatory purposes.

Principle 10. Responsibility and Accountability: As the controller, or processor, you must comply with the law and must be able to prove it. Also, you must review and improve the effectiveness of the protection measures implemented for the personal data you process.

Legal Basis for Processing of Personal Data

Under the LGPD (Article 7), personal data can only be processed if there's at least one legal basis for doing so.

The legal bases are

- Consent of the data subject

- Compliance with the laws or regulations

- Public interest

- Research studies

- Contract execution

- Judicial, administrative, or arbitration procedures

- Protection of life or physical safety of persons

- Protection of health

- Legitimate interests of the controller or a third party

- Credit protection

Consent

According to LGPD (Articles 8, 11, and 14):

1. Consent to process data must be freely given and for specific purposes by data subjects.

2. Data subjects must be informed of their right to withdraw their consent.

3. Consent must be explicit in the case of sensitive personal data or transborder dataflows.

4. The controller shall bear the burden of proving that consent was obtained in accordance with the provisions of this law, etc.

5. The processing of sensitive personal data shall only occur certain cases, such as consent of data subjects, controller's compliance with a legal or regulatory obligation, shared processing of data by public entities, etc.

Transparency

Under the LPD (Article 9), data subjects have the right to be informed of the nature of the processing of their personal data in a clear, adequate, and overt way.

Data Security Measures and Breach Notification

According to LGPD (Articles 46 to 49), both controllers and processors must adopt technical and administrative data security measures to protect personal data from unauthorized access, accidents, destruction, and loss and must develop secure information systems.

Also, the controller must communicate to the national authority and to the data subjects the occurrence of a security incident that may create risk or relevant damage to the data subjects and other relevant details, etc.

For more details, also see my LGPD privacy books in the "Additional Resources" section.

Recommended Actions

The following actions are recommended to help you understand better the control requirements of ISO 27001 and data privacy regulations (e.g., GDPR and LGPD). These are

Action 1: Review and ensure you understand the control requirements of ISO 27001 (the International Information Security Standard) and how it may affect your operations, processing of data, and activities.

Action 2: Review and ensure you understand the aspects of major privacy regulations (e.g., GDPR and LGPD) and how they may affect your operations, processing of data, and activities.

Conclusion

Understanding the ISO 27K and privacy information security and privacy regulation requirements completes the achievement of the second milestone (Understand ISO 27K and Privacy Requirements) of Phase A (Obligations and Requirements Comprehension).

CHAPTER 3

Information Security and Data Breach Response Framework

This chapter supports you to achieve your third milestone (Ensure effective IT Governance and Privacy Controls) of Phase B (Security and Privacy Framework Assurance). It contains a description of the required steps and actions that must be executed to establish an effective security incident and data breach response framework.

Introduction

The first thing you need to do in preparing to respond to information security incidents and data breaches effectively is to establish a set of governance controls or measures, such as establish response teams, train staff, and develop policies and procedures, etc.

The following actions are designed to achieve this, as best as possible.

Steps to Establish Security Incident and Data Breach Response Framework

Step 1: Define security roles and responsibilities

Step 2: Ensure effective implementation of IT policies

Step 3: Train employees on information security

Step 4: Prepare for data breach management

Step 5: Train employees on data privacy

Step 6: Understand data flows

Step 7: Review measures, technology, and third parties

These are described next.

Step 1: Define Security Roles and Responsibilities

Action 1.1: Define the roles and responsibilities of staff, and appoint the executives who will be responsible for comprehensively and effectively managing IT security incidents.

Action 1.2: Define the roles and responsibilities of all users and management regarding everyone's responsibility to report all security incidents to the appropriate authorities.

Three examples of these (board security responsibilities, senior management security responsibilities, and information security manager-job description) are outlined next.

Example 1: Board Security Responsibilities (BSR)

BSR1: Become informed about information security.

BSR2: Set direction, i.e., drive policy and strategy and define a global risk profile.

BSR3: Provide resources to information security efforts.

BSR4: Assign responsibilities to management.

BSR5: Set security priorities.

BSR6: Support change.

BSR7: Define cultural values related to threats and risk awareness.

BSR8: Obtain assurance from internal or external auditors.

BSR9: Ensure that management makes security investments, as required.

BSR10: Monitor improvements and reports on security program effectiveness.

BSR11: Provide oversight for the development of a security and control framework that consists of standards, measures, practices, and procedures, after a relevant security policy has been approved by the board and related roles and responsibilities assigned.

BSR12: Set direction for the creation of a security policy, with business input and risk assessment.

Example 2: Senior Management Security Responsibilities (MSR)

MSR1: Ensure that individual roles, responsibilities, and authority related to information security are clearly communicated and understood by all.

MSR2: Ensure that threats and vulnerabilities be identified, analyzed, and monitored and industry practices used for due care.

MSR3: Ensure the set-up of an information security infrastructure.

MSR4: Set direction to ensure that resources are available to allow for prioritization of possible controls and countermeasures implement accordingly on a timely basis and maintained effectively.

MSR5: Establish monitoring measures to detect and ensure correction of security breaches, so all actual and suspected breaches are promptly identified, investigated, and acted upon, and to ensure ongoing compliance with policy, standards and minimum acceptable security practices.

MSR6: Ensure that periodic security and audit reviews and tests are conducted.

MSR7: Ensure processes are developed that will support the implementation of and intrusion detection and incident response system.

MSR8: Ensure performance and security metrics are developed to ensure that information is protected, correct skills are on hand to operate information systems securely, and security incidents are responded to on a timely basis.

MSR9: Ensure staff are aware and trained on security, as needed.

MSR10: Ensure that security is considered an integral part of the systems development life cycle process and is explicitly addressed during each phase of the process.

Example 3: Information Security Manager-Job Description

Main Duties: The main responsibilities and duties of an InfoSec manager usually include the following:

Security Policies: Provide guidance, lead, and manage, as required, the design, development, implementation, documentation, and maintenance aspects of information security policies, procedures, and standards across all enterprise departments and functions.

Security Management

- Create and facilitate an enterprise information security steering committee to help guide strategic information security needs.

  Plan and coordinate security staff, activities, and operations for regular and specific events.

- Coordinate security staff when responding to emergencies and alarms.

- Review reports on security incidents and data breaches.

- Investigate and resolve issues, as required.

- Monitor the internal control systems to ensure that appropriate access levels are maintained.

  Create reports for management on security status.

- Assist in system and software architecture and design to ensure that information assets are appropriately secure at all times.

  Provide guidance, management, and oversight for intrusion detection and response.

  Collaborate with the IT function to ensure that the information technology department is adequately skilled and engaged in company emergency plans as appropriate.

- Attend meetings with other managers to determine security operational needs.

- Create and maintain all information system and software security certificate activities.

IT Disaster Recovery: Provide guidance, lead, and manage, as required, the development, implementation, and maintenance aspects of the enterprise information systems disaster recovery plan considering the existing company business continuity plans.

Security Training and Awareness

- Initiate, facilitate, enable, and promote training and communication activities and procedures to create information security awareness throughout the enterprise.

- Recruit, train, and supervise security officers and guards.

- Attend conferences and training seminars as required to maintain proficiency.

Performance Management

- Review the performance of all information security staff.

- Control budgets for security operations.

- Monitor security expenses.

- Issue security performance reports to senior management of the enterprise.

Monitoring

- Monitor and audit compliance to all information security procedures and policies, and ensure consistency of internal controls across all enterprise departments.

- Monitor changes in local, national, and international regulations and accreditation standards affecting information security, and make recommendations to the senior company management on the need for policy changes.

Risk Assessment: Independently perform risk assessments and work closely with the company internal audit staff or other third-party auditors to respond to any audit findings that require action.

Step 2: Ensure Effective Implementation of IT Policies

Action 2.1: Confirm the good implementation and operation of all IT policies and procedures, such as access policies, intrusion detection, IT assets ownership and control, data classification, IT disaster recovery and IT backup policies, and malware protection, etc.

Action 2.2: Ensure threat intelligence (role, function, policy, etc.) is implemented effectively. See Appendix A.

Action 2.3: Ensure logging and IT security monitoring procedures operate as best as possible. See Appendix B.

Action 2.4: Confirm the good implementation and operation of security equipment and software (firewalls, intrusion detection systems, etc.). See Appendix C.

Action 2.5: Confirm the good implementation and operation of all corporate HR security-related controls. An example of these includes[1]

- Employee verification checks procedure
- Employee confidentiality and privacy agreement
- Staff education and training policy
- Employee disciplinary policy, etc.

Step 3: Train Employees on Information Security

Action 3.1: Train your employees on all aspects and concepts of information security and how to respond to security incidents effectively.

Action 3.2: You need to make sure employees have the required IT and digital skills, understand the usual IT and Digital concepts and terms, and know what constitutes a security incident and that security is more than just managing any potential damages to information resources.

Action 3.3: Your employees should know who to contact in the event of an information security incident.

For more details, see Appendices D, E, and F.

Step 4: Prepare for Data Breach Management

Action 4.1: Establish Your Personal Data Breach Response Group

Ensure the establishment and operation of a cross-functional Personal Data Breach Incident Response Group.

Ensure this group reviews, approves, and participates in the execution of the response actions for each identified Personal Data Breach.

Action 4.2: Review Standards and Regulations

Review the requirements of the relevant international security standards related to your company.

Review the requirements of the relevant international and local privacy regimes related to your company.

See Chapter 2 for more details.

Step 5: Train Employees on Data Privacy

Action 5.1: Train Employees on Data Privacy

Educating employees about data confidentiality, data security, and reporting and responding to data breach incidents is the right first action. You need to make sure employees have the required IT and digital skills, understand the usual IT and digital concepts and terms, and know what constitutes a personal data breach and that it is more than just losing personal data.

Action 5.2: Ensure Employees Know Who to Contact

Also, your employees should know who to contact in the event of a personal data breach.

For more details, see Appendices D, E, F, and G.

Step 6: Understand Data Flows

You need to have a clear and complete picture of your company's data flows. It is therefore important to know and assess the data flows in your company and the relative sensitivity of the different sets of personal data processed.

Step 7: Review Measures, Technology, and Third Parties

Action 7.1: Evaluate Security Measures

With a picture of the data flows, you should also evaluate the security measures taken into account to see and assess how vulnerable your company is.

Action 7.2: Review the Technology Used

Depending on how vulnerable your company is, you may also need to install a set of technological tools, such as data loss prevention, intrusion detection and prevention, encryption, and pseudonymization, etc.

Action 7.3: Review Processing of Data by Third Parties

When your data is processed by third-party companies (processors), you must review all agreements with them regarding security obligations and data breach notification requirements. It is contractually recommended that you require your service providers to notify you of any security incidents as soon as possible, but ultimately within certain hours of becoming aware of the incident in order to be able to meet the relevant privacy requirements.

Conclusion

Establishing an effective security incident and data breach response framework completes the achievement of the third milestone (Ensure Effective IT Governance and Privacy Controls) of Phase B (Security and Privacy Framework Assurance).

CHAPTER 4

Managing Information Security Incidents

This chapter supports you to achieve your fourth milestone (Manage Security Incident Responses) of Phase C (Security Incident and Breach Response Management). It contains an approach to manage information security incidents of three stages (discovery and analysis, remediation, and documentation) and ten steps (e.g., discover security incidents, communicate security incidents, and analyze and evaluate security incidents).

The steps to investigate cybercrimes are included in Chapter 5, while the steps to manage data breaches are described in Chapter 6.

Information Security Incident Management Approach

A usual security incident management approach includes the following three stages and ten steps:

Stage 1: Discovery and analysis

Step 1: Discover security incidents

Step 2: Communicate security incidents

Step 3: Analyze and evaluate security incidents

Step 4: Determine response strategy to security incidents

Stage 2: Remediation

Step 5: Contain damage due to security incidents

Step 6: Prevent reinfection

Step 7: Restore affected systems

Stage 3: Documentation

Step 8: Document the incident

Step 9: Report the incident

Step 10: Preserve evidence

Stage 1: Discovery and Analysis

Step 1: Discover Security Incidents

Action 1.1: Ensure you implement an incident reporting policy and that all parties know it and are using it as well as the relevant form to report incidents.

See also Appendices H and I.

Action 1.2: Ensure the following are aware how to discover and report a security incident when something is wrong or suspicious. These include

1. The IT support office

2. The intrusion detection system

3. Any user of IT services

4. A system administrator

5. A firewall administrator

6. A business partner

7. A customer

8. A security monitoring team member

9. The external security support service or one of its members

10. The data recorded in the transaction or event recording mechanisms (i.e., logs)

Step 2: Communicate Security Incidents

Action 2.1: Communication is vital to incident response. It is important to review all issues surrounding an incident so that communication is most appropriate and effective in resolving the specific incident for the company.

Action 2.2: You should carefully consider the following aspects of IT security incident communication:

(1) To determine the circumstances when employees, customers and partners can or cannot be informed about which incidents.

(2) To limit the disclosure of information about each incident on a need-to-know basis.

(3) To determine the procedures for the control of communication with the mass media.

(4) To determine the procedure for safe communication during an incident.

(5) To determine the information, during a security emergency, with the relevant technology providers.

(6) To have the contact details of customers, in case they are affected by a security incident.

Action 2.3: Inform the police or other authorities in case of prosecution of the intruder or for reasons of compliance with the rules of the national authorities (e.g., Stock Exchange, Central Bank, and Securities and Exchange Commission).

If the security incident involves also a data breach, you will have to inform (usually done by the company's privacy officer) the relevant data privacy or data protection authority.

Step 3: Analyze and Evaluate Security Incidents

Action 3.1: Determine the appropriate response, including assessing the incident and providing a response to each type of incident. Use the following questions:

(1) Is it the real incident?

(2) Is the incident still ongoing?

(3) What data or property is threatened and how critical is it?

(4) What are the business implications if the attack succeeds?

(5) Which compromised systems are they targeting, and where are they located on the network?

(6) Is the incident within the trusted network?

Another useful evaluation procedure proposed by Data Guard[1] includes the following steps:

Step 1: Secure the scene

Step 2: Gather information

Step 3: Evaluate the situation

Step 4: Identify the cause

Step 5: Analyze the impact

Step 6: Determine the severity

Step 7: Consider contributing factors

Action 3.2: Determine the appropriate response for each category of IT security incidents.

Category 1: Unauthorized access/malicious code/attempted access.

Response: The response in all three cases must be immediate because immediate actions must be taken for the specific incident and longer-term actions to avoid other such security incidents.

Reporting: Reporting to higher levels of company management must be done within one hour of discovery, reporting, or detection of the incident.

Category 2: Denial of service (DoS). An attack that successfully prevents or interferes with the normal authorized functionality of networks, systems, or applications by depleting company resources.

Response: The response must be immediate because immediate actions must be taken for the specific incident and longer-term actions to prevent other such security incidents.

Reporting: Reporting to higher levels of company management must be done within two hours of discovery, reporting, or detection of the incident.

Category 3: Improper use. A person violates the company's accepted IT security policies, procedures, and practices.

Response: The response must be within the day or as soon as possible because immediate actions must be taken for the specific incident and person and longer-term actions to prevent other such security incidents.

Reporting: Reporting to higher levels of company management must be done on a weekly basis from the discovery, reporting, or detection of the incident.

Category 4: Unconfirmed. Unconfirmed security events that are potentially malicious or anomalous activity deemed by IT or other business function executives to warrant further investigation.

Response: The response should be within the week, as immediate actions need to be taken for the specific incident and person and longer-term actions to prevent other such security incidents.

Reporting: Reporting to higher levels of company management must be done on a weekly basis from the investigation of the incident.

Category 5: Network defense drills and intrusion testing. This category is used during drills, defense, and intrusion testing by authorized individuals on the company's network and other infrastructure.

Response: According to the agreed schedule.

Reporting: When the tests are completed.

Based on all of the above (questions, research, IT security incident categorization), you can then (next step) determine your most correct response to resolving the security incident. If the security incident also relates to data breaches, take also appropriate privacy actions (as per Chapter 6).

For examples of security incidents and data breaches, see Chapter 1.

Step 4: Determine Response Strategy to Security Incidents

Action 4.1: Determine a response strategy based on what was mentioned in step 3 and judging by the following: Is the response urgent? Can the incident be quickly isolated? Will our reaction have an impact on the attacker and do we care?

Acting quickly to reduce the actual and potential effects of an attack can make the difference between a minor and a major event. The exact answer will depend on your company and the nature of the attack you face.

However, the following priorities (P) can be a starting point:

P1. Human Life: The protection of human life and the safety of people. This should, of course, always be your first priority.

P2. Sensitive Data: Protecting classified, personal, and sensitive data is your second priority. As part of your incident response planning, you should clearly define what data are categorized as classified, personal, or sensitive. This will enable you to prioritize your responses and comply better with the relevant data protection regulation (e.g., GDPR for EU).

P3. Other Data: Protecting other company data is your third priority. Protect other company assets, including financial, scientific, customer, and other business data.

P4. Information Assets: Protecting information assets is your fourth priority. Protect hardware and software against attack. This includes protection against loss or corruption of system files and physical damage to hardware (equipment). Computer system failure can lead to costly damage and malfunctions.

Stage 2: Remediation

Step 5: Contain Damage due to Security Incidents

There are a number of measures you can take to contain harm, limit the damage, and minimize the risk to your environment.

At a minimum, you should consider the following:

(1) **Avoidance Tactics:** Try to avoid letting the attacker know that you know and are aware of their activities. This can be difficult because a few basic answers could alert the attackers. For example, if there is an emergency incident response team meeting or you need to change all passwords immediately, then all internal hackers (or insider attackers) could know that you are aware of an incident.

(2) **Cost Comparison:** Compare the cost of system shutdown at risk versus the risk of continuing to operate. In the vast majority of cases, you should immediately disconnect the system from the network. However, you may have service agreements with your customers and may even incur the potential for further damage. In these circumstances, you may choose to maintain an online system with limited connectivity in order to gather additional evidence during the ongoing attack.

(3) **Access Point:** Determine the access point used by the attacker and implement security measures to prevent future attacks.

(4) **Rebuild System:** Consider rebuilding a new system with new hard drives or even new network equipment.

2. Existing hard drives should be removed and preserved to be used as evidence if you decide to prosecute the attackers.

3. Make sure you change any local passwords.

4. You should also change your administrative and other system passwords.

Step 6: Prevent Reinfection

Action 6.1: Determine how the penetration occurred.

Action 6.2: Determine the source of the intrusion (if it was email, etc.).

Action 6.3: Determine if staff training was inadequate.

Action 6.4: Specify the intrusion port, etc.

Action 6.5: Take steps to prevent immediate reinfection, which may include one or more of the following:

Close a port on a firewall.

Repair the affected system.

Shut down the infected system until it can be reinstalled.

Restore the infected system (with a fresh install) and its data from a backup.

Make sure backups were correct before infection.

Change your email settings to prevent an attachment type from being possible through the email system.

Plan for additional user training.

Disable unused services on the affected system, etc.

Step 7: Restore Affected Systems

Actions to properly restore affected systems to their original state include the following:

Action 7.1: Preserve evidence against the attacker by backing up log files or possibly the entire system.

Action 7.2: Reinstall the affected system or systems from scratch and restore data from backups if necessary.

Action 7.3: Make users change their passwords.

Action 7.4: Make the system more resilient by disabling or uninstalling unused services.

Action 7.5: Make sure the system or systems are fully patched.

Action 7.6: Ensure that virus protection and intrusion detection mechanisms are fully operational.

Action 7.7: Make sure the logging system is in full operation.

If the security incident also relates to data breaches, take also appropriate privacy actions (as per Chapter 6).

Stage 3: Documentation

Step 8: Document the Incident

There should be a record of each event (incident) in a relevant file, which will include the following:

(1) Date and time when the incident took place

(2) Details of the person who reported it

For more details, see Appendix I.

Step 9: Report the Incident

There should be a process for drawing up a report that will report by time period (per month, quarter, year, etc.) and according to applicable provisions of the company and regulatory authorities (e.g., National Stock Exchange), personal data legal framework (e.g., GDPR for EU, HIPAA, Sarbanes-Oxley), or industrial standards (ISO, Payment Card Industry-Data Security Standards, etc.) all company security incidents.

Step 10: Preserve Evidence

In many cases, if your environment has been deliberately attacked, you may want to take legal action against the perpetrators.

In order to maintain this option, you should gather and preserve the evidence that can be used against them, even if you ultimately do not seek such action.

For these reasons, you should

1. Back up the systems before performing any actions that could affect data integrity relative to the original state.

2. Keep all written and electronic communication in a special file.

For more details, see also Chapter 5.

Conclusion

Establishing an effective security incident response process completes the achievement of the fourth milestone (Manage Security Incident Responses) of Phase C (Security Incident and Breach Response Management).

CHAPTER 5

Investigating Cybercrimes

This chapter supports you to achieve your fifth milestone (Investigate Cybercrimes) of Phase C (Security Incident and Breach Response Management). It contains a seven-step methodology that may be used to investigate cybercrimes, such as step 1: conduct initial assessment; step 2: confirm investigator readiness, etc. These investigation steps support the actions of step 10 (preserve evidence) of "Managing Information Security Incidents" (see Chapter 4) and step 3 (investigate data breaches) of "Managing Data Breaches" (see Chapter 6).

Introduction

Investigation of a cybercrime is a process consisting of investigating, analyzing, and recovering forensic data for digital evidence of a crime. A cybercrime is a crime that involves a computer and a network. The computer may have been used in the commission of a crime, or it may be the target.

Cybercrime Investigation Steps

Cybercrime investigators typically follow a standard set of investigation and examination steps and actions[1], as described below.

© The Editor(s) (if applicable) and The Author(s),
under exclusive license to APress Media, LLC, part of Springer Nature 2024
J. Kyriazoglou, *Information Security Incident and Data Breach Management*,
https://doi.org/10.1007/979-8-8688-0870-8_5

Step 1: Conduct Initial Assessment

Action 1: Provide company resources and guidelines on the investigation of the specific security incident.

Action 2: Assess any risks related to the investigation, provide instructions, and resolve any issues, as required.

Action 3: Resolve any potential threats related to the investigator upon entering your company's premises and decide how best to address them.

Action 4: Be aware of health and safety issues, conflict of interest issues, and potential business risks (financial, reputational, etc.) before approving the investigation of the incident.

Step 2: Confirm Investigator Readiness and Tools

Investigator readiness is an important and sometimes overlooked stage of the investigation and examination process. This includes

Action 1: Confirming that the investigator has received the appropriate training

Action 2: Ensuring that they have the right equipment, other tools, and the appropriate investigation software and that they are trained to use them in actual field cases

These tools include network analysis tools, malware analysis tools, digital forensics software, password recovery tools, social media analysis tools, etc.

In addition to these tools, cybercrime investigators may use various other techniques to gather evidence and identify suspects.

These techniques can include conducting interviews with witnesses, reviewing surveillance footage, and analyzing financial records to track the flow of money. They may also use social engineering techniques to gather information about suspects, such as posing as potential victims or using fake social media profiles to gain access to information, etc.

Action 3: Ensuring that they have the right knowledge and familiarity with the security and privacy regulations and legislation

Action 4: Ensuring that they have the right top management support to carry out the required tasks effectively

Step 3: Ensure Evidence Collection

Action 1: The investigator makes a digital copy of the device's storage media.

Action 2: After the copy, the original media and the device are locked in a safe place to maintain their excellent condition. All investigation and research are done on the digital copy.

Action 3: If this investigation is to be done on site and not in a crime lab computer, then this step will also include identifying and devices that can store crime scene evidence.

Action 4: Interviews or meetings should also be held with personnel who may hold information relevant to the examination (which could include computer end users and the administrator and IT service provider, etc.).

Action 5: The collection phase also includes marking and bagging the crime scene evidence and sealing it in numbered bags.

Action 6: Finally, the issue of safe transport of the material to the researcher's laboratory must also be considered.

Step 4: Conduct Incident Analysis

The analysis depends on the specifics of each investigation. The investigator usually provides feedback to the company manager or officer during the analysis, and from this dialog, the analysis can take a different path or be limited to specific areas.

The analysis must be accurate, unbiased, repeatable, and completed within the available timescales and available resources. There are many tools available for cybercrime analysis. Each investigator should use whatever tool they are comfortable with and knows very well, as long as they can justify their choice.

The electronic evidence sources that the investigator should consider for searching electronic evidence are hard disk drives and solid-state disks, removable media, memory cards, USB data storage devices, data storage tape disks, peripheral devices, tablet devices, mobile telephones, photo and video recordings, etc.

Analyzing log files is essential particularly in cases of attacks against systems. The investigator should extract not only allocated log files but also traces of deleted and unallocated log files.

In situations where the investigator finds traces of cloud services being used on a computer system, this might mean that evidential data might not only be stored on that machine but also on a remote storage. The support of the cloud services provider should be requested in this case.

Step 5: Craft and Issue Report

This step usually involves the investigator writing a structured report of their findings, addressing the issues in the initial guidelines, along with any subsequent guidelines, etc. It will also cover any other information that the investigator considers relevant, with the examination.

The report should be written with the reader in mind. The r investigator should also be prepared to attend meetings to discuss the issues of the report.

Step 6: Review Findings and Issues

As with the readiness step, the review step is often overlooked or ignored. An investigator review can be simple and quick and can start during any of the above steps. It can include a basic analysis of what went wrong, what went right, and how learning from this can lead to incorporating changes and improvements throughout the whole process.

Step 7: Improve Methodology

Any lessons learned from this investigation process should be applied to the next investigation and examination and improve all steps of the methodology accordingly.

Conclusion

Effective investigation of cybercrimes completes the achievement of the fifth milestone (Investigate Cybercrimes) of Phase C (Security Incident and Breach Response Management).

CHAPTER 6

Managing Data Breaches

This chapter supports you to achieve your sixth milestone (Manage Data Breach Responses) of Phase C (Security Incident and Breach Response Management). It contains a seven-step methodology that may be used to support you in managing data breaches, such as step 1: ensure data breach management readiness; step 2: identify data breaches; step 3: investigate data breaches, etc.

Introduction

A personal data breach is usually defined as "a breach of security leading to the accidental or unlawful destruction, loss, alteration, unauthorized disclosure of, or access to, personal data transmitted, stored or otherwise processed in connection with the provision of a public electronic communications service." A personal data breach may mean that someone other than the data controller gets unauthorized access to personal data. But a personal data breach can also occur if there is unauthorized access within an organization, or if a data controller's own employee accidentally alters or deletes personal data.

In contrast to the typical security incident response, which concerns a broader range of incidents affecting information security, this control uses the term Personal Data Breach Incident to describe only those incidents that relate to personal data.

Security Obligations

Security plays a primary role in all privacy and data protection regulatory regimes (e.g., EU's GDPR, Brazil's LGPD, Canada's PIPEDA, China's Personal Information Protection Law (PIPL)[1]). The principle of transparency in all privacy regulations allows individuals to exercise their rights and get assurance by organizations that their personal data are always secure. For example, appropriate mechanisms for international data transfers or other types of personal data processing by processors are of little value to individuals if their data are not secure. A lack of consumer trust has been identified as a key risk to the development of the digital single market, and a number of high-profile data breaches have exacerbated the situation. Therefore, all privacy regulations have made data security a critical part of everyday life.

Security obligations apply to both controllers (companies holding personal data) and processors (companies processing personal data). This makes sense in today's world, where service providers can have a large influence on the security measures taken and have already established complex subcontracting agreements that they may find impractical or undesirable to seek to modify. With rules directly applicable to both controllers and processors offering goods or services all over the world, any company that processes personal data must have an idea of the security obligations that apply to it.

Both controllers and processors are obliged to "apply appropriate technical and organizational measures" taking into account "the development of technology and implementation costs" and "the nature, scope, context and purpose of the processing and the risk or varying probability and severity to the rights and freedoms of natural persons."

In addition, privacy regulations require controllers to only engage processors that provide "adequate guarantees for the implementation of appropriate technical and organizational measures" in order to meet the requirements of the relevant data protection or privacy regime and protect the rights of individuals (data subjects).

These provide specific guidelines for the types of security actions that may be considered appropriate for the risk. These guidelines include

- The ability to ensure the continued confidentiality, integrity, availability, and resilience of processing systems and services

- The ability to promptly restore availability and access to personal data in the event of a physical or technical event, such as a data breach

- Pseudonymization and encryption of personal data

- A process of regularly testing and evaluating the effectiveness of technical and organizational measures to ensure the security of processing

The above shows that "security" is not only about external threats, but also covers issues of continued operation.

Notification Obligations

All privacy regulations include specific breach notification guidelines. According to these, so-called "personal data breaches" should be notified, by the controllers to the supervisory authorities and in some cases also to the affected individuals.

The following steps will support your efforts to manage data breaches in the best way possible.

An example of such a procedure is described next.

Data Breach Management Procedure

This procedure includes the following steps and actions:

Step 1: Ensure data breach management readiness

Step 2: Identify data breaches

Step 3: Investigate data breaches

Step 4: Respond to data breaches

Step 5: Preserve evidence

Step 6: Notify authorities and individuals

Step 7: Maintain data breach documentation

Step 1: Ensure Data Breach Management Readiness

Ensure all actions to prepare your organization to manage data breaches (as per Chapter 3, step 4: prepare for data breach management; step 5: train employees on data privacy; step 6: understand data flows, and step 7: review measures, technology and third parties) have been successfully carried out.

Step 2: Identify Data Breaches

Action 2.1: Ensure All Staff Know When an Incident Is a Personal Data Breach

Breach of personal data may involve loss of personal data or illegal access or processing of personal data. Only if an incident actually caused a breach of personal data does the mandatory notification obligation apply. For example, lost USB sticks, stolen laptops, malware infections, or hacked databases containing personal data are considered personal data breaches.

A threat or a weakness in security measures, such as weak passwords or outdated firewalls, is not considered a personal data breach, as long as no personal data has been leaked. Therefore, these issues regarding security measures do not fall under the obligation of mandatory notification.

Action 2.2: Report Data Breaches

Ensure when a non-IT employee becomes aware of a potential or real data breach, or the IT team detects a data breach by the monitoring activities, they use the breach form (see Appendix J) and report it to the DPO (data protection or privacy officer) and the security incident and data breach response teams.

Step 3: Investigate Data Breaches

Action 3.1: Investigate the Source of the Breach

What is the source of the personal data breach? For example, is it a stolen device or is it an internal security measure that has been breached?

You may also use the steps described in Chapter 4 or 5.

Action 3.2: Determine the Number of People Affected

How many people are affected by the personal data breach and is the data breach likely to result in a risk to the rights and freedoms of the people affected? For example, a breach of a customer database could likely have a serious impact on the privacy of many people. On the other hand, a breach involving only a customer's business contact information may only have a minimal impact.

Action 3.3: Research What Type of Data Are Involved

Does the compromised personal data contain sensitive data? For example, credit card details, passport numbers or health data, etc.

Action 3.4: Review Protection Techniques of Breached Data

Is the compromised personal data encrypted or secured in a way that makes third-party evaluation impossible? For example, if sufficient encryption is used or the data is sufficiently transformed using "data hashing," "data salting" techniques, etc., it can be assumed that third parties will not have access to the personal data.

Action 3.5: Review Mitigation Measures

What measures were taken to mitigate (further) the loss of personal data? For example, if it is possible to delete (wipe) all personal data remotely, so as to avoid the loss of personal data or to gain access to a compromised (hacked) database to mitigate further losses, etc.

Action 3.6: Investigate Parties Involved

Which parties are involved in the data breach? For example, if a common database is hacked, it cannot be ruled out that many parties will be involved and/or affected by the data breach.

Step 4: Respond to Data Breaches

Action 4.1: Contain the Breach

Ensure you contain the breach effectively to prevent further damage. You need to isolate and secure the affected systems, devices, and networks and stop any unauthorized access or data transfer.

This will include one or more of the following:

(1)   Disable (do not delete) remote access capability and wireless access points. Change all account passwords and disable (not delete) noncritical accounts. Document old passwords for later analysis.

(2)   Disconnect from the Internet by pulling the network cable from the firewall/router to stop the bleeding of data.

(3)   Document the entire incident. Document how you learned of the suspected breach, the date and time you were notified, how you were notified, what you were told in the notification, all actions you take between now and the end of the incident, date and time you disconnected systems from the Internet, disabled remote access, changed credentials/ passwords, and all other system hardening or remediation steps taken, etc.

(4) Disable (do not delete) remote access capability and wireless access points.

(5) Change all account passwords and disable (not delete) noncritical accounts. Document old passwords for later analysis. Change access control credentials (usernames and passwords) and implement better or more complex passwords.

(6) Segregate all hardware devices in the payment process from other business critical devices. Relocate these devices to a separate network subnet and keep them powered on to preserve volatile data.

(7) Quarantine instead of deleting (removing) identified malware found by your antivirus scanner for later analysis and evidence.

(8) Preserve firewall settings, firewall logs, system logs, and security logs (take screenshots if necessary).

Action 4.2: Restore Systems

You also need to restore systems affected by a data breach.

Once you've found and secured the source of the breach, you need to bring all affected systems back online. Make sure they are secure against future attacks by reaching full compliance with the relevant privacy regulation and information security used by the company.

Action 4.3: Assess Potential Harm

Ensure you implement a data protection risk assessment process to determine the extent of potential harm, embarrassment, inconvenience, or unfairness to affected individuals.

Step 5: Preserve Evidence

You also need to preserve any evidence that might help you trace the breach or support legal action. Before you begin preserving electronic or digital evidence, it's important to identify what evidence is relevant to your case. This will help you focus your preservation efforts and ensure that you don't miss any important evidence.

It's important not to alter or delete any electronic or digital evidence during the preservation process. Even minor changes to electronic evidence can be detected and can raise questions about the authenticity of the evidence. Make sure to make copies of any relevant evidence and preserve the original in its original format.

Forensic tools can be useful for preserving electronic evidence. These tools can help you create a forensically sound copy of the evidence and can ensure that the original evidence remains intact. In addition, forensic tools can help you identify metadata and other information that may be relevant to your case.

It's also important to secure your electronic evidence to prevent unauthorized access or tampering. This can include locking up physical devices, restricting access to electronic devices, and using strong passwords and encryption.

Step 6: Notify Authorities and Individuals

Action 6.1: Investigate the Notification Obligation to the Supervisory Authority

The data protection or privacy supervisory authority must be informed by the controller of any personal data breach that results or may result in a "risk to the rights and freedoms of natural persons." This should be assessed on a case-by-case basis.

For example, you should notify the appropriate supervisory authority of the loss of customer information when the breach leaves individuals open to identity theft.

On the other hand, the loss or improper modification of an internal phone book, for example, would not normally satisfy this threshold.

In this regard, it is appropriate to know the answers to the above questions and to know the reasonable consequences that the breach may have (for example, lead to discrimination, damage to reputation, financial loss, loss of confidentiality or any other significant economic or social disadvantage).

If all the information is not yet available, the controller should inform the supervisory authority. If necessary, the notification can be amended at a later stage when the full details are known or the notification can be withdrawn if it is not necessary.

When notification to the supervisory authority is required, it is recommended to first check if the supervisory authority uses a standard breach notification form and use it accordingly.

The usual information communicated includes

- The scope and nature of the personal data breach, including the categories and number of data subjects and relevant data files

- The name and contact details of the data protection officer (if any) or other point of contact where further information can be obtained

- Description of the possible consequences of the personal data breach

- A description of the measures taken or proposed to be taken to address the breach, including measures to mitigate any adverse effects, etc.

Action 6.2: Investigate Your Duty to Notify Individuals

When a breach of personal data is likely to result in a "high risk" to the rights and freedoms of individuals, you should inform those directly concerned. You should consult your relevant privacy regulation to get a full understanding of what "high risk" means and the complete guidelines on notification to individuals.

If the persons concerned need to be informed, you should provide at least the following information in clear and plain language:

- The scope and nature of the personal data breach

- The name and contact details of the data protection officer (if any) or other point of contact where further information can be obtained

- Description of the possible consequences of the personal data breach

- A description of the measures taken or proposed to be taken to address the breach, including measures to mitigate any adverse effects (e.g., contact your credit card provider, change your password)

Step 7: Maintain Data Breach Documentation

Action 7.1: Create and Maintain a Personal Data Breach Register

Controllers are required to document any personal data breaches, which includes at least information about the events surrounding the personal data breach, the impact of the breach, and the efforts and remedial measures taken. A Personal Data Breach Register may be used for this purpose.

Action 7.2: Maintain Data Breach Documentation Securely

Ensure your DPO documents any personal data breaches, comprising the facts relating to the personal data breach, its effects, and the remedial action taken.

Ensure this documentation is safely kept to enable the supervisory authority to verify compliance with the relevant privacy regime.

Documentation of any communication with regulatory authorities and affected individuals is also recommended.

In addition, in the event that it was decided not to notify the supervisory authorities and/or those affected, it is recommended to keep a record of the events and the reasons why this decision was taken as the supervisory authority can initiate an audit or information request at any time.

Conclusion

Effective management of data breaches completes the achievement of the sixth milestone (Manage Data Breach Responses) of Phase C (Security Incident and Breach Response Management).

CHAPTER 7

Improving Security Incident and Data Breach Responses

This chapter supports you to achieve your seventh milestone (Improve Information Incident and Breach Response Process) of Phase D (Security and Breach Response Process Evaluation). It contains a five-step process that may be used to support you in improving security incident and data breach responses, such as step 1: assess security incident cost; step 2: review processes; step 3: assess data breach management measures, etc.

Summary

This phase (Security and Breach Response Process Evaluation) includes the following six steps:

> **Step 1:** Assess information governance controls framework
>
> **Step 2:** Assess security incident cost
>
> **Step 3:** Review information incident response process and measures

Step 4: Assess data breach management process and measures

Step 5: Review lessons learned

Step 6: Improve processes and measures

These are described below.

Improvement Steps

Step 1: Assess Information Governance Controls Framework[1]

Issue 1: Information Security Incident and Data Breach Policies

Q1: Does the organization have effective policies and procedures to rapidly identify information security and data breaches?

Q2: Are all employees trained and empowered to monitor, report, and respond to information security incidents and data breaches?

Q3: Are information security and data breach responses integrated well into IT operations?

Q4: Are the organization's cyber and data breach responses effectively aligned to business requirements ensuring that all functions of the business understand their roles in the relevant response plans?

Q5: Do the organization's response plans match up with appropriate corporate threat intelligence?

Q6: Are information security and data privacy risks characterized in a way that is consistent with most likely attacks?

Q7: Are appropriate information security products installed and used?

Issue 2: Risk Management

Q1: Has the organization established a cybersecurity and data privacy risk committee?

Q2: Do board directors discuss cybersecurity and data privacy risks at every board meeting?

Q3: Are all directors educated and comfortable to discuss cybersecurity and data privacy risks?

Q4: Are potential cybersecurity and data privacy risks considered from the outset of all business initiatives from corporate strategy to new types of customer interaction?

Q5: Are new kinds of risk associated with emerging digital business initiatives considered?

Q6: Are corporate resources optimized by prioritizing along two dimensions: what's most valuable and what's most vulnerable?

Q7: Does the board ensure the quality of risk policies and practices around the organization's approach to information governance so that all assets are protected appropriately?

Issue 3: Human Resource Management

Q1: Are continuous enterprise-wide cybersecurity and data privacy awareness, education, and training programs implemented?

Q2: Are all relevant staff trained on information security and data privacy and protection laws and regulations and relevant topics?

Q3: Are these programs reviewed and improved as required?

Issue 4: Third-Party Relationships

Q1: Are all business partner relationships for potential cybersecurity vulnerabilities reviewed as required?

Q2: Are the relevant information security and data privacy controls implemented as per relevant information security and data privacy and protection laws and regulations?

Issue 5: Information Security Incident and Data Breach Response Management

Q1: Does the organization have first-class information security incident and data breach response controls?

Q2: Are all organization employees a part of the relevant response plan and team (information security incident, data breach)?

Q3: Are information security incident and data breach response plans continually reviewed and improved, as needed?

Step 2: Assess Security Incident Cost

Estimate the cost of the damage, as well as the cost of containment efforts, for each security incident, by following the actions below:

Action 1: Estimate the direct costs of the incident. Direct costs are the expenses that are directly related to the incident response and recovery, such as labor, equipment, software, consultants, and legal fees. Calculate these costs on the basis of the duration and impact of the incident.

Action 2: Estimate indirect costs of the incident. Indirect costs are the expenses that are not directly related to the incident response and recovery, but are caused by the incident, such as lost revenue, lost productivity, customer churn, regulatory fines, and reputation damage. Calculate these costs on the basis of the duration and impact of the incident.

Action 3: Estimate the intangible costs of the incident. Intangible costs are the costs that are difficult to quantify, but have a significant effect on the business, such as customer satisfaction, brand loyalty, employee morale, and competitive advantage. These intangible costs should be estimated on the basis of the potential value and growth of the business.

Action 4: Estimate the opportunity costs of the incident. Opportunity costs are the costs that represent the benefits that could have been gained if the incident did not occur, such as new customers, new markets, new products, or new partnerships. These opportunity costs should be estimated on the basis of the potential value and growth of the business.

Step 3: Review Information Incident Response Process and Measures

Action 1: Consider whether an additional policy or control could have prevented the invasion.

Action 2: Investigate if a procedure or policy was not followed that allowed the intrusion and could be changed to ensure the procedure or policy is followed in the future.

Action 3: Was the response to the incident appropriate? How could it be improved?

Action 4: Was the improvement or recovery done on time?

Action 5: Were incident response procedures followed in detail and was the entire situation covered? How can they be improved?

Action 6: Have changes been made to systems, equipment, software, and procedures to prevent reinfection of the current infection?

Action 7: What lessons have been learned from this experience?

Step 4: Assess Data Breach Management Process and Measures

The accountability principle of the privacy regimes requires data controllers to be responsible and able to "prove" compliance with data protection principles, which include security obligations.

Given the accountability requirement, it is recommended that you document what your company has done to prevent future personal data breaches from the same source and that you regularly review and update your breach detection, investigation, and internal reporting processes.

Step 5: Review Lessons

Review lessons learned complete documentation that could not be prepared during the security incident or breach response process. Investigate the security incident and data breach further to identify their full scope, how they were contained and eradicated, what was done to recover the attacked systems, areas where the security breach response teams were effective, and areas that require improvement.

The above learning process should include the following:

Action 1. Meeting: Conduct a meeting with the cybersecurity or data breach team and major/ critical users together after each security incident or data breach.

Action 2. Review: Review the data, impact, results, and anything else that is relevant (e.g., security report) of the security incident or data breach and how they were resolved.

Action 3. Recovery: Ensure all systems and data have been recovered or treated appropriately (no contaminations exist).

Action 4. Changes: Consider changes to existing information security or data protection controls or adding new security and data protection controls.

Action 5. Awareness: Keep all users and interested parties aware of what has taken place, which security and data protection controls have changed or are to be implemented, other good practices to be implemented and what to avoid, etc.

Action 6. Sharing: Ensure you share lessons learned with other trusted third parties, including partners, government agencies, regulators, industry or professional associations, etc., as applicable.

Action 7. Documentation: Document all issues discussed and actions/practices/controls to be changed, added, etc.

Step 6: Improve Processes and Measures

Depending on all results of the above actions carried out, you may improve one or more information security process and compliance measures, such as retrain staff, install more antimalware protection software, add more firewalls, redesign your network, upgrade security policies and procedures, backups, etc.

In addition to all the above, you should regularly review and update your security measures and the training provided to employees on data security and the handling of personal data breaches

Also, you should review breach responses and update data protection policies and procedures so the breach cannot repeat itself.

Conclusion

Effective improvement of the security incident and data breach response processes completes the achievement of the seventh milestone (Improve Information Incident and Breach Response Process) of Phase D (Security and Breach Response Process Evaluation).

Appendices

These appendices contain policies, plans, and forms that may be used to support you in managing and improving your security incident and data breach responses.

© The Editor(s) (if applicable) and The Author(s),
under exclusive license to APress Media, LLC, part of Springer Nature 2024
J. Kyriazoglou, *Information Security Incident and Data Breach Management*,
https://doi.org/10.1007/979-8-8688-0870-8

APPENDIX A

Threat Intelligence Policy

Objective

The objective of this policy is to define the requirements for the proper establishment, enablement, facilitation, and operation of the threat intelligence program of company "XXX".

Applicability

This policy is applicable to all company employees, partners, contractors, consultants, temporary, and other workers, including any and all personnel affiliated with third parties, including vendors and external services providers (termed "users"). Also, this policy applies to all information. Data, IT assets, resources, network, equipment, or systems owned, used, or leased by the company, as well as personally owned computers and devices connected remotely to the company network.

Threat Definition

"Threat" according to ISO is "the potential cause of an unwanted incident, which can result in harm to a system or organization."

Threat Intelligence Layers

Threat intelligence can be divided into three layers, which should all be considered:

(1) Strategic threat intelligence: exchange of high-level information about the changing threat landscape (e.g., types of attackers or types of attacks)

(2) Tactical threat intelligence: information about attacker methodologies, tools, and technologies involved

(3) Operational threat intelligence: details about specific attacks, including technical indicators

Threat Intelligence Policy Guidelines (TIG)

TIG01: This policy is established and is designed to operate within the framework of the company's business intelligence process.

TIG02: A process and relevant effective organizational and technical resources and controls will be established and implemented for threat intelligence activities and should include

2.1: Establishing objectives for threat intelligence production

2.2: Identifying threats

2.3: Identifying, vetting, and selecting internal and external information sources that are necessary and appropriate to provide information required for the production of threat intelligence

2.4: Collecting information from selected sources, which can be internal (e.g., compliance of policies, procedures, log monitoring, security events, and data breaches) and external (e.g., security organizations, research entities, industrial forums, and professional associations)

2.5: Processing information collected to prepare it for analysis (e.g., by translating, formatting, or corroborating information)

2.6: Analyzing information to understand how it relates and is meaningful to the organization

2.7: Communicating and sharing it to relevant individuals within the company and third parties and groups, as authorized, in a format that can be understood by all concerned. Also getting feedback and review comments and acting on them

2.8: Analyzing collected information about existing or emerging threats in order to (a) facilitate informed actions to prevent the threats from causing harm to the organization and (b) reduce the impact of such threats

2.9: Ensuring that threat intelligence is (a) relevant (i.e., related to the protection of the organization); (b) insightful (i.e., providing the organization with an accurate and detailed understanding of the threat landscape); (c) contextual, to provide situational awareness (i.e., adding context to the information based on the time of events, where they occur, previous experiences and prevalence in similar organizations); and (d) actionable (i.e., the organization can act on information quickly and effectively)

2.10: Ensuring that threat intelligence is effectively analyzed and later used (a) by implementing processes to include information gathered from threat intelligence sources into the organization's information security risk management processes; (b) as additional input to technical preventive and detective controls like firewalls, intrusion detection system, or antimalware solutions; and (c) as input to the information security test processes and techniques.

TIG03: Appropriate and specific staff with defined responsibilities will be allocated to threat intelligence and should include business intelligence manager, CISO, IT manager, security team personnel, DPO, information systems owners, a senior management member, representatives of the legal and compliance functions, etc.

TIG04: A budget will be prepared, approved, and executed for installation of special tools for threat intelligence, staff training, acquiring external threat information, etc.

TIG05: A threat escalation classification scheme (e.g., low, moderate, high, and impact) will be established to categorize all threats and take appropriate actions to remedy the actual or potential impacts to the company

TIG06: The company's IT function is assigned to verify compliance to this policy and make the necessary reports to top management for further action, as required.

TIG07: This policy and the complementary procedures, practices, and security improvement controls (e.g., xxx) will be reviewed and improved on an annual basis, and on an ad hoc basis, as required.

Violation of This Policy

If any user is found to be in violation of the IT security policy, the company will take disciplinary action, including the restriction and possible loss of access privileges and other more serious consequences, up to and including suspension or termination from the company and other legal ramifications, as stated by national laws and government regulations.

APPENDIX B

IT Logging Policy

Objective

The objective of this policy is to describe how logging will function for information technology (IT) resources, systems, and services of the company.

Applicability and Enforcement

This policy applies to any company-owned IT resource, system, or service that collects, stores, processes, or transmits company data regardless of where these data are located.

Additionally, this policy applies to end user devices (desktop, laptop, tablet, mobile or other networked device, etc.) that are critical to the operation and maintenance of all IT systems.

Violation of this policy may result in loss of access and disciplinary action up to and including termination of employment or services of third parties, as well as other legal actions, as needed.

© The Editor(s) (if applicable) and The Author(s),
under exclusive license to APress Media, LLC, part of Springer Nature 2024
J. Kyriazoglou, *Information Security Incident and Data Breach Management*,
https://doi.org/10.1007/979-8-8688-0870-8

Responsibilities

It is the responsibility of all company staff to ensure that the controls described in this document are implemented.

IT management with the full collaboration of all business managers and the approval of the general manager, CEO, or the board will decide, on the basis of risk assessment, regulatory requirements or business needs, which IT resources (systems, hardware, networks, applications, data, devices, etc.) will be using processes and tools to record activities and events on logs.

IT management is responsible to ensure that all technical controls related to logging are implemented, reviewed, and improved and that all staff are trained on these controls.

Company departments undergo periodic audits. These audits sometimes include an analysis of the processes and controls used by company departments to secure and manage end user devices, servers, and applications. Each department, with the full support of IT, is responsible for remediation of any findings of noncompliance with this policy within the time frame agreed to with the auditors.

Principles (P)

P1: All selected resources and systems shall record and retain logging information sufficient to answer the following questions (Q):

Q1: What event, activity, or transaction was performed?

Q2: Who or what performed the event, activity, or transaction?

Q3: From where or on what system the event, activity, or transaction was performed?

Q4: When was the event, activity, or transaction performed?

Q5: With what tool(s) was the event, activity, or transaction performed?

Q6: What was the status (e.g., success, failure), outcome, or result of the event, activity, or transaction?

Q7: Which entity (employee, customer, anonymous user, etc.) and data were impacted?

P2: The log management system shall support the formatting and storage of audit logs in such a way as to ensure the integrity of the logs and to support company-level analysis and reporting.

P3: Logs shall be reviewed and acted upon to resolve any security or other events or issues.

P4: All IT resources, systems, and devices will be configured to enable logging to be performed.

P5: An Intrusion Detection or Prevention System (IDS/IPS), antivirus system, or antispyware system will be obtained, deployed, and used.

P6: Logs produced by the company IT resources should be protected and examined regularly to protect company IT resources and data. At a minimum, systems containing high risk data should have their logs reviewed weekly or more frequently if required by law, regulation, contract provisions, or industry standards.

P7: Logs shall be retained a minimum of six months or longer depending on retention requirements mandated by company policy, laws, or regulations.

What (W) Is to Be Logged

Logs for the following events, activities, and transactions shall be created, depending on the risk assessment basis:

> **W1:** Create, read, update, or delete high or medium risk information and data.
>
> **W2:** Create, read, update, or delete authentication and authorization information such as user credential, passwords, login, and logout.

W3: Initiate or accept a network connection.

W4: Grant, modify, or revoke access rights, including adding a new user or group, changing user privilege levels, changing file permissions, changing database object permissions, changing firewall rules, and user password changes.

W5: Manage (initiate, change, delete) configurations on systems, networks, services, hardware, devices, etc.

W6: Install software, patches, and updates.

W7: Manage application and network processes (e.g., startup, shutdown, or restart, abort, failure, abnormal end).

Contents of the Log

Logs shall contain at least the following elements (E):

E1: Type of action (e.g., initiate, authorize, create, read, update, delete, and accept)

E2: System, application, network, or device component performing the action

E3: Identifiers requesting the action (e.g., computer name and IP address, username, computer program name, file or data base name accessed or updated)

E4: Before and after images or values when action involves updating a complete record or data element

E5: Date and time the action was performed, including relevant time zone information

E6: Whether the action was allowed or denied by access control mechanisms

E7: Description and reason codes of why the action was denied by the access control mechanism

Log Retention by Default: Logs will be retained a minimum of 90 days and no longer than six months. Exceptions to this will be allowed by recommendation from the IT security office or other vice president for IT designee when different log retention requirements are mandated by university policy; federal, state, or local laws; or regulations.

APPENDIX C

Minimum IT Security and Privacy Controls

Minimum IT Security Controls

Controls for Servers (SC)

SC1. Inventory: Record all servers in the IT Inventory.

SC2. Patching: Apply high severity security patches ASAP.

SC3. Vulnerability Management: Perform a monthly scan. Remediate severity 4 and 5 vulnerabilities within 14 days of discovery and severity 3 vulnerabilities within 60 days.

SC4. Access Control: Implement user authorization access policy. Review existing accounts and privileges quarterly. Enforce password complexity.

SC5. Authentication: Implement a two- or even three-step authentication process for all interactive user and administrator logins.

SC6. Firewall: Enable host-based firewall in default deny mode and permit the minimum necessary services.

SC7. Malware Protection: Install antivirus and other advanced protection software. Review alerts as they are received.

SC8. Intrusion Detection: Install and operate intrusion prevention system. Review alerts as they are received.

SC9. Physical Protection: Place system hardware in a data center.

SC10. Data Security Controls: Implement privacy and security policies and procedures to comply with GDPR.

Controls for Applications (AC)

AC1. Inventory: Record all applications in the IT Inventory. Update records every quarter.

AC2. Patching: Apply high severity security patches ASAP.

AC3. Vulnerability Management: Perform a monthly scan. Remediate severity 4 and 5 vulnerabilities within 14 days of discovery and severity 3 vulnerabilities within 60 days.

AC4. Access Control: Implement user authorization access policy. Review existing accounts and privileges quarterly. Enforce password complexity.

AC5. Authentication: Implement a two- or even three-step authentication process for all interactive user and administrator logins to applications.

AC6. Firewall: Permit the minimum necessary services through the network firewall.

AC7. Secure Software Development: Include privacy and security controls as a design requirement. Review all code and correct identified security flaws prior to deployment. Use of static code analysis tools recommended.

AC8. Backups: Back up application data at least weekly. Encrypt backup data in transit and at rest.

AC9. Developer Training: Ensure development staff attend at least one privacy and one security training course annually.

AC10. Data Security Controls: Implement privacy and security policies and procedures to comply with GDPR.

Controls for End Point Devices (EC)

EC1. Inventory: Record all devices in the IT inventory.

EC2. Patching: Apply security patches ASAP. Use a supported OS version.

EC3. Whole Disk Encryption: Enable encryption software especially for personal data.

EC4. Malware Protection: Install antivirus.

EC5. Backups: Back up user data at least daily. Encrypt backup data in transit and at rest.

Minimum Privacy Controls

1. Information security policy

2. Cookies policy

3. Website privacy policy

4. Employees privacy policy

5. Data retention/removal policy

6. Data quality policy

7. Backup/recovery policy

8. Malware protection policy

9. Encryption policy

10. Pseudonymization/anonymization/data aggregation policy

11. Consent management system

12. Subject rights satisfaction system

13. Security incident management system

14. Data breach management system

15. Privacy education and training policy

16. DPIA methodology

17. Data protection audit methodology

18. Security and privacy controls in information systems plan

19. PD inventory

20. IT assets inventory

APPENDIX D

Staff Education and Training Policy

Overview

The company's training policy, <COMPANY LOGO, TITLE, BUSINESS ADDRESS, WEBSITE: XXX, etc.> (hereinafter referred to as "company"), contains the framework and general rules, characteristics, and limitations that determine the training of all employees in all company levels on issues of company management and operations such as (but not limited to) privacy, information security, quality, etc.

Objective

The objective of this policy is to define the methodology followed for the training of the company's personnel, in order to ensure that all employees have the required skills to perform their tasks and are aware of the requirements of the specific standards and legal and regulatory frameworks that govern the company's operations.

© The Editor(s) (if applicable) and The Author(s),
under exclusive license to APress Media, LLC, part of Springer Nature 2024
J. Kyriazoglou, *Information Security Incident and Data Breach Management*,
https://doi.org/10.1007/979-8-8688-0870-8

Applicability

This policy applies to every employee, full-time or part-time, of the company and in any case of a change in functions or legislative or regulatory frameworks or renewal of the company's standards (e.g., ISO 9001).

This policy may also be applied to temporary employees only after management approval and does not apply to external partners or other specialist consultants for service, maintenance, etc.

Policy Principles (PP)

PP1: All employees of the company are covered by this policy without discrimination of gender, position in the hierarchy, etc.

PP2: Managers must evaluate the success of education and training efforts. They should keep relevant records for reference and finding better opportunities for improvement.

PP3: All employee development efforts must respect cost and time constraints, as well as individual and business needs.

PP4: Employees should try to make the most of their education and training by studying diligently and finding ways to apply the knowledge to their work.

PP5: Employees are encouraged to utilize to their benefit the available training and education budget and time.

PP6: All education and training will follow the steps included in the "Education and Training Procedure" of the company.

Duties and Responsibilities

Chief Executive Officer (CEO)

The chief executive officer (CEO) is ultimately responsible for ensuring that this policy and the procedures that support it are implemented.

In day-to-day practice, however, this may be delegated to operational management and more specifically to the company's human resources manager.

Human Resources Manager

The executive who heads the human resources department has overall responsibility to the general manager and the company's board of directors for the implementation of this policy and its procedures.

The executive's role is also to advise the board and senior management on the risks of not providing adequate training to the company's staff, to manage all aspects of the execution of the training of the company's staff as well as to provide timely and accurate information on the mandatory and required company-wide training requirements.

Data Protection Officer

The data protection officer has at least the following duties regarding the training of the company's staff in matters of personal data protection:

a) Informs and advises the controller (general manager, etc.) or the processor and the employees who process data of their obligations arising from the relevant data protection or privacy regulation and from other provisions of the State regarding data protection

b)   Monitors compliance with the relevant privacy regime (e.g., GDPR for EU and LGPD for Brazil) with other provisions of the State on data protection

c)   Monitors compliance with the relevant privacy and security policies of the controller or processor in relation to the protection of personal data, including delegation of powers, the awareness and training of the employees who participate in the processing operations, and the relevant controls, etc.

Directors

The managers of the company's operational departments will ensure that all their staff attend the planned training on the subjects approved according to the needs and requirements of the specific departments of the company.

The head of each department reviews the education and training certificates of their department staff against the job requirements to determine if additional training is needed to perform a staff task.

Staff

All company employees must comply with all requirements set forth in this policy and its procedures.

Trainers

Trainers (inside or outside the company) are responsible for preparing the training material and conducting the specific seminars in a natural way or providing another form of training to the company's staff.

Instructors are required to

- Express themselves clearly and understandably

- Have the necessary technical knowledge of the object or subject

- Know how to use written material and audiovisual aids

- Encourage the participation of the trainees

- Monitor the performance of trainees and evaluate their progress, etc.

Identification and Recognition of Training Needs

All company personnel, senior leadership, data protection officer, employees, department managers, and the human resources department must work together to develop a culture of continuous professional development.

It is the responsibility of each employee to seek out new learning opportunities.

It is the responsibility of the data protection officer to coordinate and oversee the training of all staff in matters of personal data protection.

It is the responsibility of the manager of each department to guide their teams and identify the development needs of the employees they manage.

The training needs may concern issues in the employees' area of responsibility or be related to

- The information security management system

- Quality and safety standards, hygiene, etc.

- Data protection

- The internal control system

- Fraud prevention

- Electronic crime

- Legislation on labor, tax and other issues, etc.

Training Planning

Staff training is planned by the data protection officer for personal data. Training for other issues are planned by the heads of the company's operational departments in collaboration with the human resources manager based on identified needs and the availability of relevant programs.

An annual training program is drawn up, submitted to the general manager (CEO) for approval no later than the end of <month XXX> each year and states:

- The subject of education or training

- The time (start, duration) of the training

- The form of education

- The person in charge, if it is internal training or the external organization

If extraordinary needs or opportunities arise, it is possible to provide training outside the program.

For the selection of participants, the established training needs and the ability of the candidates to benefit (previous education, experience, etc.) are taken into account.

Method of Providing Training

Training can be done inside or outside the company. Participants are notified by the head of the department. Participation in training programs outside the company by an external organization or holding seminars at the company's offices is approved by the CEO.

After the end of the external training, the employee

- Delivers training program documentation to human resources manager for filing

- Delivers a copy of the certificate that may have been obtained to the head of his department, who communicates it to the human resources manager for filing, etc.

In-house training is provided by company staff or external trainers. Instructors are responsible for preparing the training material.

Types of Education

Training can be provided in the following ways.

Group Training

This type of training is preferred when the number of trainees is large and the purpose is to provide technical or other information, to solve technical problems, or to explain a method or policy or procedure.

On the Job Training

This type of training is preferred when the number of trainees per training session is small, the subject of training involves some skill, and knowledge is most easily imparted by personal demonstration and participation of the trainee.

The training includes indicatively

- Explaining what learners need to learn

- Demonstration of the work by the instructor

- Execution of the same task by the trainee

- Analysis by the instructor, guidance and re-execution if necessary.

Participation in a Conference (Conference Attendance)

This type of training is used to provide general information to participants on general or specific topics presented by expert analysts on the specific topics. Minutes and notes must be kept by the staff participating in them and any printed or audiovisual material collected as well as the notes made available to all staff in the company, for full information of all.

Self-Administered Training

This type of training is used for appropriate subjects and when no tangible experience is required. Printed or audiovisual materials must be available and some objective way of measuring learning performance must be established.

Application and Compliance Framework

Compliance: Any violations, partial or full noncompliance, etc., of the rules, concepts, and principles embodied in this document by the employees will not be tolerated by the company.

Correction: The company will quickly take all necessary administrative and legal measures to correct any issue that may arise.

Violation: Anyone found to have violated or failed to comply with these principles (as set forth herein) may be subject to various penalties. These are defined in the internal operating regulations, policies, and procedures of the company and in other national legislative and regulatory frameworks. Indicatively, these penalties include the interruption of work, the dismissal of an employee, the cancellation of the work and contractual arrangements of partners, the resignation of a member of the board of directors, etc.

APPENDIX E

IT and Digital Skills Checklist

Basic or Minimum Required Skills (BS)

BS1. Hardware: Use a keyboard and operating touchscreen technology. Turn on the device and enter any account information as required. Use settings in menus to change device display to make content easier to read. Keep login information for a device and any websites secure, not shared with anyone or written down and left prominently near your device, etc.

BS2. Software: Use standard office software (e.g., Microsoft Word/Excel/PowerPoint), managing files on laptops, privacy settings on mobile phones, etc.

BS3. Online Operations. Execute basic online operations (e.g., email, search, or completing an online form, etc.).

BS4. Company Systems. Access and navigate company's network, web content, and application systems.

BS5. IT Policies. Comply with company's IT (password, access control, disaster recovery, etc.) and social media policies, procedures, and practices.

BS6. Internet Code. Apply rules of ethical conduct when using digital technologies and when interacting in digital environments.

BS7. Protection of ICT Devices: Understand the risks and threats in digital environments and know how to protect devices and digital content.

BS8. Personal Data Protection: Understand the company's privacy policy and controls and know how to apply them in order to protect personal data and privacy in digital environments.

BS9. Intellectual Property: Understand the application and validity of copyright and licensing of data, information, and digital content.

BS10. Solving Technical Problems: Identify technical problems during the operation of devices, teleworking tasks, and the use of digital environments and obtain support from the company's IT function or other authorized parties to solve them effectively.

Intermediate or Second-Level Skills (IS)

Know how to

IS1: Explore, search, and filter data, information, and digital content.

IS2: Access and navigate digital environments.

IS3: Analyze and evaluate data, information, and digital content in a critical way.

IS4: Organize, manage, store, and retrieve data, information, and digital content.

IS5: Communicate and interact through various digital technologies and understand the appropriate means of digital communication.

IS6: Share data, information, and digital content with third parties through appropriate digital technologies.

IS7: Use public and private digital services to participate in public discussions.

IS8: Use digital tools and technologies for collaborative processes.

IS9: Synchronize and share information across different devices including computers, tablets, and mobile phones.

IS10: Use the Internet to find sources of help for a range of activities.

IS11: Use chat facilities on websites to help you solve problems.

IS12: Use online tutorials, FAQs, and advice forums to solve problems and improve your skills in using devices, software, and applications.

IS13: Use appropriate software to present information and manipulate and analyze data to help solve problems at work.

IS14: Protect your health and well-being while working with digital technologies and avoid health risks and threats to your physical and mental well-being when using digital technologies.

Advanced or Third-Level Skills (AS)

Know how to

AS1: Create and edit digital content in different formats.

AS2: Modify, improve, and integrate information into existing content to create new, original, and relevant digital content.

AS3: Use digital design and data visualization tools to analyze complex data to help management make vital business decisions.

AS4: Use the tools of desktop publishing, digital graphic design, and digital marketing.

AS5: Interpret data visualizations, such as graphs and charts, etc.

AS6: Use programming languages to develop advanced online, web, mobile, and other related applications.

AS7: Assess the environmental impacts of digital technologies and their use.

APPENDIX F

Glossary of IT Concepts and Terms

This appendix contains the description of several of concepts and terms used in this book as well as numerous common computer and Internet terms.

For a more comprehensive IT glossary of about 500 terms and concepts, see https://www.morebooks.de/shop-ui/shop/product/9786205523520.

Algorithm: An "algorithm" is the process or sequence of steps used to solve a problem.

Antivirus Program: Programs capable of detecting, removing, and protecting against various forms of malicious code or malware, including viruses, worms, Trojan horses, spyware, and adware.

Application Software: Application software is a program or set of programs that does a real job for the end user. It is primarily created to perform a specific task for a user.

Application software acts as an intermediary between the end user and the system software. This type of software is written using a high-level language such as C, Java, VB. Net, etc. It is made for business needs and for specific users (e.g., Payroll Processing, Financial Accounting).

Backup: A backup is a copy of computer data and/or computer software taken and stored elsewhere so that it may be used to restore the original after a data or software loss event.

Cloud Computing: The practice of using a network of remote servers hosted on the Internet to store, manage, and process data, rather than a local server or a personal computer.

Computer Virus: A computer virus is a type of malicious code or program that is written to change the way a computer works and is designed to spread from one computer to another. When running, it replicates itself by modifying other computer programs and entering its own code. If this reproduction succeeds, the affected areas are said to be "infected" with a computer virus, etc.

Cookies: A special file, used by web servers, in order to retrieve and store information for the identification of visitors to each website.

Data: Data are facts or numbers in primitive form and represent measurements or natural phenomena or elements of interest to a person or a business entity.

Data are considered as pieces of reality that represent another reality, as well as symbols that represent the real world.

Database: The term "database" describes the organization of files containing data or information objects organized in a hierarchical or relational format with pointers, keywords, and other mechanisms for faster access, maintenance, and retrieval of data and information by users, through the special software "data base management system."

Data Protection: Data protection is usually defined as the legislation for the protection of personal data, which is collected, managed, processed, and stored by electronic or "automated" means and technologies (computerized or automated systems, digital media) or by procedures of a manual system archiving (manual system). In the European Union, the legislation includes the General Data Protection Regulation (GDPR) and other complementary laws.

Electronic Mail (Email): Email is the electronic transfer of nonstandard messages between two points (or individuals) that are connected to a telecommunication network either internally (intranet) or externally (via the Internet).

Encryption: Encryption is the process of encoding information. This process converts the original representation of the information, known as plaintext, into an alternative form known as ciphertext. Ideally, only authorized parties can decipher a ciphertext back to plaintext and access the original information. Encryption does not itself prevent interference but denies the intelligible content to a would-be interceptor.

For technical reasons, an encryption scheme usually uses a pseudorandom encryption key generated by an algorithm. It is possible to decrypt the message without possessing the key but, for a well-designed encryption scheme, considerable computational resources and skills are required. An authorized recipient can easily decrypt the message with the key provided by the originator to recipients but not to unauthorized users.

Firewall: The set of objects (software and hardware) used to prevent users from changing, viewing, or copying private information over the Internet. It can be a program or computer, which acts as a "guard," controlling any incoming or outgoing data, for security reasons.

Information: Information is data in a form that can be used in a decision-making activity by the company's management. Information is considered to be the set of business data used to support the operation of the business, to make faster decisions, and to achieve its financial, operational, and business objectives more correctly, quickly, and effectively.

Information System: An information system or application system is an organized set of five interacting entities that processes data and produces information on behalf of a Company or Organization. These five components are people, processes, data, application software, and hardware.

Information System Security: Information system security is the organized framework of approaches, concepts, principles, policies, procedures, equipment, software, techniques, and measures required to protect the components of the information system, the data it retains, but also the system as a whole, from any intentional or accidental threat.

Information Technology (IT): IT is not an extension of mathematics and electrical engineering, and it is not just computer programming. It is the science that deals with the collection, processing and storage of data and information, and the publication of various analyses and specific results of logical operations on data and information. It uses the technologies of computers and telecommunications and methods of the sciences of business administration and systems analysis.

Internet: The Internet is best described as "a global system of interconnected computer networks." It is a network of millions of interconnected computers that extends to almost every corner of the globe and provides its services to millions of users.

Password: A series of characters (letters, numbers, special symbols, etc.) that are required to be entered to authorize access to a computer system, device, application, etc. These are used to allow online access to authorized users only.

Privacy: The right of the individual concerning all his personal data to decide for himself when, how, and to what extent they will be transmitted to others and not to be used without his explicit approval.

Privacy has been recognized as a fundamental human right and in a democratic society it is protected by various data protection laws, such as the European Union General Data Protection Regulation (GDPR).

System Software: System software is a set of programs that control and manage the functions of the computer hardware. It also helps applications run properly. System software is designed to control the functionality and operation of a computer system. System software makes running a computer faster, more efficient, and more secure, for example, operating system, programming languages (computer languages), communications software, system utilities.

APPENDIX G

Privacy Awareness, Communication, and Training Plan

Action #1: Carry Out Ongoing Data Privacy Training for the Privacy Office

Through ongoing data privacy training, continuing professional education, guest speakers, research on privacy development and trends, subscriptions to privacy magazines and specialist law firms, attendance and participation in data protection and privacy conferences, etc., for the data protection or data privacy officer, the company's privacy function is provided with adequate training and kept up to date on key data privacy trends and best practices for the organization.

This benefits the company by having the data protection or data privacy officer versed on best policies, procedures, and practices which in turn lead to increased and better knowledge of privacy for the organization.

© The Editor(s) (if applicable) and The Author(s),
under exclusive license to APress Media, LLC, part of Springer Nature 2024
J. Kyriazoglou, *Information Security Incident and Data Breach Management*,
https://doi.org/10.1007/979-8-8688-0870-8

Action #2: Execute Basic Privacy Training for Staff

Your company or organization develops, implements, and maintains a basic data privacy training program for its new and existing corporate staff (board, management, and employees).

Processes are in place to ensure that privacy training content is updated and enhanced as required; privacy training takes place on a regular basis, i.e., yearly; privacy learning objectives are achieved; and privacy training attendance is documented in the personnel files.

The company also ensures the re-enforcement of this privacy training program by guiding staff to maintain an understanding of the company's data protection and privacy policies and practices.

Action #3: Execute Additional Privacy Training for New Needs

Data protection and privacy needs and requirements may change over time as new systems are implemented, new rules are applied, etc. Corporate staff, because of these, may require additional data privacy training due to the privacy-sensitive nature of these new developments. This is required to ensure that staff obtain an increased knowledge of the organization's data protection and privacy policies and practices.

To facilitate this, your company conducts an assessment of the job responsibilities that impact data privacy to ensure that relevant data privacy requirements for jobs are included in this further training.

It also provides regular refresher privacy training to ensure that employees understand the organization's privacy policies and practices and remain ahead of any new data protection and privacy developments that may impact the existing company privacy policies, procedures, and practices.

Action #4: Include Data Privacy Training into Other Corporate Training

Your company or organization incorporates data protection and privacy training into other corporate training programs, such as human resource training, customer support training, security training, and new employee orientation training, etc.

This is a must as the integration of data protection and privacy training with other company training programs allows the specific company or organization to ensure that data privacy and protection messaging is aligned between all corporate training programs.

Action #5: Maintain Data Privacy Awareness

Your company or organization establishes a data privacy portal, a privacy blog, or privacy FAQs, as well as posters and videos. It may also conduct privacy awareness events (e.g., an annual data privacy day/week) and deliver a data privacy newsletter, or incorporate data privacy into existing corporate communications

These are used to communicate privacy information to all members within your organization and to all visitors of your company website. The privacy portal may contain links to online training material, data privacy documents, and relevant privacy information. This awareness information should be kept up to date by the data protection or privacy officer and supported by the IT and other business functions, as deemed necessary (e.g., customer support and HR).

Action #6: Maintain Data Privacy Professional Certification for Privacy Personnel

There are various privacy certifications provided to privacy individuals by numerous certification organizations across the world, such as

1. CIPP/C (for Canada), CIPP/E (for Europe), CIPP/G (for US government), and CIPP/US (for US private sector) provided by the International Association of Privacy Professionals)

2. CHPC provided by the Compliance Certification Board

3. HCISPP by the International Information System Security Certification Consortium, Inc.

4. CHPS provided by the American Health Information Management Association

Having your privacy individuals certified in their field demonstrates your company's commitment to data protection and privacy. Continuing professional education ("CPE") allows your data privacy specialists to keep abreast of current data privacy trends, information, and best practices while maintaining professional certification. A minimum set of hours each year is a requirement for privacy professionals who wish to maintain their privacy professional designation.

Action #7: Measure Data Privacy Awareness and Training Activities

Measuring the participation of your staff in data privacy awareness, communications, and training actions demonstrates your company's commitment to data protection and privacy.

The measure of "participation" could be achieved through various means: audit reviews of PACT actions, participants taking a test containing data protection and privacy questions, recording the names of participants attending data privacy training, etc.

Each of these methods proves that data privacy awareness, communications, and training have taken place.

APPENDIX H

Information Security Incident Reporting Policy

This appendix describes a typical Information Security Incident Reporting Policy.

Objective

The objective of this policy is to define the requirements for the proper reporting of a security incident so that appropriate remedial actions can be undertaken.

Applicability

This policy is applicable to all Company employees, partners, contractors, consultants, temporary, and other workers, including any and all personnel affiliated with third parties, including vendors and external services providers (termed "users"). Also, this policy applies to all

© The Editor(s) (if applicable) and The Author(s),
under exclusive license to APress Media, LLC, part of Springer Nature 2024
J. Kyriazoglou, *Information Security Incident and Data Breach Management*,
https://doi.org/10.1007/979-8-8688-0870-8

information. Data, IT assets, resources, network, equipment, or systems owned, used, or leased by the company, as well as, personally owned computers and devices connected remotely to the company network.

Definitions

An information security incident is (a) an attempted, suspected, unsuccessful, successful, or imminent threat of unauthorized access, use, disclosure, breach, modification, or destruction of information; (b) interference with information technology and related communications operations; or (c) significant violation of company security policies, procedures, and practices.

Examples of Information Security Incidents

Examples of information security incidents (SIE) include the following:

SIE 1: Suspected or actual breaches, compromises, or other unauthorized access to company systems, information, data, applications, or accounts

SIE 2: Loss or theft of computer equipment or other data storage devices and media (e.g., laptop, USB drive, personally owned device used for company work) used to store personal or potentially sensitive information

SIE 3: Theft or loss of IT and related equipment, devices, and media

SIE 4: Computer system or website real or potential intrusion

SIE 5: Unauthorized or inappropriate disclosure of company data

SIE 6: Unauthorized changes to computers or software (operating system, application, office, etc.)

SIE 7: Denial-of-service attack or an attack that prevents or impairs the authorized use of networks, systems, or applications

SIE 8: Interference with the intended use or inappropriate or improper usage of IT resources, including security policies, procedures, and practices

Policy Principles (PP)

PP1: All users of company IT and related information resources and assets must report all information security incidents immediately to their manager and the IT manager or CISO of the company.

PP2: If the security incident involves a data breach, the privacy officer of the company must also be informed.

PP3: All users should use the relevant form to report a security incident.

PP4: To avoid inadvertent violations of regulations and laws, users and department managers may not release information, electronic devices, or electronic media to any outside entity, including law enforcement organizations, before getting express management approval.

PP5: Information related to company security information security incidents is classified as sensitive. When company staff report, track, and respond to information security incidents, they must protect and keep confidential any sensitive information.

PP6: The company CISO or IT manager, depending on board approval, is responsible to interpret and implement this policy.

PP7: All company staff are responsible to report all security incidents immediately or as soon as possible after the event or incident.

Violation of This Policy

If any user is found to be in violation of the **Information Security Incident Reporting Policy,** the company will take disciplinary action, including the restriction and possible loss of access privileges and other more serious consequences, up to and including suspension or termination from the company and other legal ramifications, as stated by national laws and government regulations.

APPENDIX I

Information Security Incident Reporting Form

This appendix describes a typical Information Security Incident Reporting Form.

1. Incident number: xxx

2. Contact details of person reporting incident

2.1. Name and surname of person: <e.g.: John Smith>

2.2. Position or role: <e.g.: Accounting system user>

2.3. Phone number: <office or other phone, i.e., cell number, etc.>

2.4. E-mail: <the reporting person e-mail address>

2.5. Location: <mailing address, office room number>

Note   Repeat above for each person, if this incident involves more persons.

---

3. Suggested severity level: <indicate which: Low, Medium, High, Critical>

4. Type of incident: Note all types that apply:

- Physical Break-in: ___(Yes/No/NA)

- Policy Violation: ___(Yes/No/NA)

- Lost Equipment: ___(Yes/No/NA)

- Theft: ___(Yes/No/NA)

- Compromised System: ___(Yes/No/NA). Also list which system or systems were impacted.

- Compromised Services: ___(Yes/No/NA). Also list services impacted.

- Compromised User Credentials: ___(Yes/No/NA)

- Social Engineering (Phishing, other): ___(Yes/No/NA)

- Network Attacks (DOS, Scanning, Sniffing): ___ (Yes/No/NA)

- Malware (Viruses, Worms, Trojans): ___(Yes/No/NA)

- Copyright Violation: ___(Yes/No/NA)

- Data Breach (physical or electronic): ___(Yes/No/NA)

- Other: <Specify>............................

5. Incident Description, Date and Time Detected
Date: <xx/month/year>
Time: <note time incident was detected>
Comments: <provide more details about the incident>. Include as much information as possible such as:

- Description of the incident (how it was detected, what occurred);

- Description of the affected resources;

- Description of the affected business functions;

- Estimated technical impact of the incident (i.e., data deleted, system crashed, application unavailable, etc.);

- Cause of the incident if known (misconfigured app, unpatched host, etc.).

6. Incident Mitigation Actions

Date: <xx/month/year>
Time: <note time incident mitigation actions were taken>
Comments: <provide more details about the mitigation actions taken regarding the incident>. Include as much information as possible such as:

- Mitigation actions taken;

- List of evidence gathered and retained;

- Include actions taken, when, and by whom and resources used, etc.;

- Total hours spent on incident handling, etc.

7. Recommendations

Comments: <provide any recommendations for future improvement actions to be taken following the resolution of the incident>

8. Additional Comments

Comments: <provide any additional notes, information or observations related to the security incident or this report>

APPENDIX J

Data Breach Reporting Form

This appendix describes an example of a Data Breach Reporting Form.

Description: This form is designed to be used by Data Subjects (employees, external users, etc.) for reporting breaches to the DPO and the IT Department, related to the personal data processed by Company (address details, phone numbers, URL, e-mail, etc.).

1. Data of person reporting a breach

Your First and Last Name: _____

Your Job Title: _____

Your Department (employees only): _____

Your E-mail: _____

Your Street Address: _____

E-mail: _____

Your Telephone: _____

Your Fax: _____

2. Environment of the breach incident

Company Name (<name of company and title>)

DATA PROTECTION OFFICER: _____

Street Address: _____

E-mail: _____

Telephone: _____

Fax: _____

3. Breach details

3.1. Provide details of the breach incident (what happened, what went wrong, and how it happened, etc.).:

……………………………………………………………………………………

3.2. Nature of the breach

(1) Breach of data confidentiality: ...YES...... NO....... Do Not Know.......

(2) Breach of data integrity: ....YES...... NO....... Do Not Know.......

(3) Breach of data availability: .....YES...... NO....... Do Not Know.......

4. Impact on your Company

4.1. High......(you have lost the ability to provide all critical services to all users)

4.2. Medium.....(you have lost the ability to provide critical services to some users)

4.3. Low.....(there is a loss of efficiency but you can still provide all critical services to all users)

4.4. Not yet known......

5. Describe how you found out about the breach

6. Describe when you found out about the breach

Date:..........................Time:............

7. Describe when the breach took place

Date:..........................Time:............

8. If there has been a delay in reporting this breach please explain why

………………………………………………………………………………

9. Provide details about categories of personal data included in the breach: e.g., Basic personal identifiers (e.g., name, contact details), Identification data (e.g. usernames, passwords), Financial data (e.g. credit card numbers, bank details), Official documents (e.g. driving license, passport), Date of birth, etc.

10. How many data subjects could be affected?........

11. List categories of data subjects affected by the breach: e.g.: Employees, Users, Patients, etc.

12. Describe the potential consequences of the breach to data subject(s): e.g.: Identity theft, fraud, property or information loss, threat to professional services, physical harm, distress, etc.).

13. Actions to deal with the data breach. Describe the actions taken or proposed to be taken to deal with the personal data breach.

14. Documents / information substantiating your report if required (List the attachments)

_____

_____

15. Declaration of truth. The information mentioned here and the submitted documents are true and valid

Date: _____

Full surname and name: _____

Identity Card or other Number (e.g., Passport): _____

Signature of: _____

End Notes

Chapter 1. Information Security and Breach Definitions and Obligations

1. For more details, see

    https://www.ibm.com/topics/
    information-security

2. For more details, see

    https://www.ibm.com/topics/threat-actor
    https://www.sentinelone.com/
    cybersecurity-101/threat-intelligence/
    threat-actor/

3. For more details, see

    https://www.ibm.com/topics/threat-actor
    https://www.sentinelone.com/cybersecurity-101/
    threat-intelligence/threat-actor/

4. See https://csrc.nist.gov/glossary/term/incident

5. See https://csrc.nist.gov/glossary/term/breach

6. For more details, see European Commission
    (commission.europa.eu)

7. For more details, see "Recommendation of the
    Council on Digital Security Risk Management,"
    OECD/LEGAL/0479, Adopted on 26/09/2022.
    https://legalinstruments.oecd.org/en/
    instruments/OECD-LEGAL-0479

Chapter 2. Summarizing ISO 27K and Major Privacy Regulations

1. For more details, see `https://www.iso.org/standard/27001`

2. For more details on GDPR, see "REGULATION (EU) 2016/679 OF THE EUROPEAN PARLIAMENT AND OF THE COUNCIL of 27 April 2016"

   `http://eur-lex.europa.eu/legal-content/EN/TXT/PDF/?uri=CELEX:32016R0679&from=EN`

   Also see my GDPR and data protection and privacy books in "Additional Resources."

3. For more details on LGPD, see `https://lgpd-brazil.info/`

   Also see my LGPD privacy books in the "Additional Resources" section.

Chapter 3: Information Security and Data Breach Response Framework

1. For more details, see my "ISO 27001: 2022 People & Physical Controls Compliance Support Tool Kit 2," available free at

   `https://www.academia.edu/113616558/ISO_27001_2022_People_and_Physical_Controls_Compliance_Support_Tool_Kit_2`

Chapter 4. Managing Information Security Incidents

1. For more details, see

   `https://www.dataguard.co.uk/blog/how-do-you-assess-an-incident/`

Chapter 5. Investigating Cybercrimes

1. The Law Enforcement Cyber Center recommends the following steps for law officers: assess the situation; conduct the initial investigation; identify possible evidence; secure devices and obtain court orders; and analyze results with prosecutor. For more details, see https://www.iacpcybercenter.org/

Chapter 6. Managing Data Breaches

1. For more details, see Craig Riddell: International Data Privacy Laws: A Guide. Published: September 18, 2023. Available at

   https://blog.netwrix.com/2023/09/18/international-data-privacy-laws/

Chapter 7. Improving Security Incident and Data Breach Responses

1. Assessment questionnaires were adopted from the material in Establishing a board-level cybersecurity review blueprint, Pages 71 to 78, in "Navigating the digital age, Cybersecurity Guide for Directors and Officers," Oct. 2015, available at https://www.nyse.com/publicdocs/Navigating_The_Digital_Age.pdf.

Additional Resources

The published works of John Kyriazoglou are listed below.

IT and Digital Age Management Books
IT Controls – English

Book 1. IT-Business Alignment (Part 1)
http://bookboon.com/en/it-business-alignment-part-i-ebook
Book 2. IT-Business Alignment (Part 2)
http://bookboon.com/en/it-business-alignment-part-ii-ebook
Book 3. IT Management Controls
https://bookboon.com/en/it-management-controls-ebook
Book 4. IT Glossary
https://www.morebooks.de/shop-ui/shop/product/9786205523520

IT Controls – Spanish

Book 1. Controles De La Seguridad De La Ti
http://bookboon.com/es/controles-de-la-seguridad-de-la-ti-ebook
Book 2. Controles del software de sistemas
https://bookboon.com/es/controles-del-software-de-sistemas-ebook

Book 3. Controles de seguridad de datos de GDPR

https://bookboon.com/es/controles-de-seguridad-de-datos-de-gdpr-ebook

Book 4. Controles de desarrollo de sistemas

https://bookboon.com/es/controles-de-desarrollo-de-sistemas-ebook

Book 5. Controles de Arquitectura Empresarial

https://bookboon.com/es/controles-de-arquitectura-empresarial-ebook

Book 6. Controles estratégicos de la TI

https://bookboon.com/es/controles-estrategicos-de-la-ti-ebook

Book 7. Controles de la organización de TI

https://bookboon.com/es/controles-de-la-organizacion-de-ti-ebook

Book 8. Controles de la administración de TI

https://bookboon.com/es/controles-de-la-administracion-de-ti-ebook

Book 9. Controles operativos del centro de datos

https://bookboon.com/es/controles-operativos-del-centro-de-datos-ebook

Book 10. Controles de aplicaciones informáticas

https://bookboon.com/es/controles-de-aplicaciones-informaticas-ebook

Book 11. Uso de Controles de TI en auditorías

https://bookboon.com/es/uso-de-controles-de-ti-en-auditoras-ebook

IT Auditing

Book 1. IT Audit Guides

https://bookboon.com/en/it-audit-guide-part-1-ebook

Book 2. IT Governance Controls - Book 2

https://bookboon.com/en/it-governance-controls-book-2-ebook

Book 3. IT Audit Execution Tools - Book 3

https://bookboon.com/en/it-audit-execution-tools-book-3-ebook

Book 4. IT Audit Support Tools 1 - Book 4

https://bookboon.com/en/it-audit-support-tools-1-book-4-ebook

Book 5. IT Audit Support Tools 2 - Book 5

https://bookboon.com/en/it-audit-support-tools-2-book-5-ebook

Digital Age Management

Book 1. Understanding Digital Age Effects

https://bookboon.com/en/understanding-digital-age-effects-ebook

Book 2. Preparing Digital Management Actions

https://bookboon.com/en/preparing-digital-management-actions-ebook

Book 3. Implementing Corporate Digital Management Actions

https://bookboon.com/en/implementing-corporate-digital-management-actions-ebook

Book 4. Implementing Personal Digital Management Actions

https://bookboon.com/en/implementing-personal-digital-management-actions-ebook

Book 5. Digital Age Management Support Tools

https://bookboon.com/en/digital-age-management-support-tools-ebook

Data Protection and Privacy Books
Data Protection and Privacy System – Five Volumes

Book 1. Data Protection and Privacy Management System – Vol. 1

https://bookboon.com/en/data-protection-and-privacy-management-system-ebook

Book 2. DP&P Strategies, Policies and Plans – Vol. 2

http://bookboon.com/en/dpp-strategies-policies-and-plans-ebook

Book 3. Data Protection Impact Assessment – Vol. 3

http://bookboon.com/en/data-protection-impact-assessment-ebook

Book 4. Data Protection Specialized Controls – Vol. 4

http://bookboon.com/en/data-protection-specialized-controls-ebook

Book 5. Security and Data Privacy Audit Questionnaires – Vol. 5

http://bookboon.com/en/security-and-data-privacy-audit-questionnaires-ebook

*LGPD Data Protection Books

Book 1. The CEO's Guide to LGPD Compliance

Author: John Kyriazoglou, Dr. Victor Rodrigues

https://bookboon.com/en/the-ceos-guide-to-lgpd-compliance-ebook

Book 2. Tools to support a more effective LGPD compliance

Author: John Kyriazoglou, Dr. Victor Rodrigues

https://bookboon.com/en/lgpd-compliance-support-tools-ebook

Book 3. O Guia do CEO para a conformidade LGPD

Author: John Kyriazoglou & Dr. Victor Rodrigues

https://bookboon.com/en/o-guia-do-ceo-para-a-conformidade-lgpd-ebook

Book 4. Ferramentas de suporte à conformidade com a LGPD

Author: John Kyriazoglou, Dr. Victor Rodrigues

https://bookboon.com/pt/ferramentas-de-suporte-a-conformidade-com-a-lgpd-ebook

GDPR Gap Analysis – Three Parts (Three E-books)

Book 1. GDPR GAP Analysis by Article

https://bookboon.com/en/gdpr-gap-analysis-by-article-ebook

Book 2. GDPR GAP Assessment Tools

https://bookboon.com/en/gdpr-gap-assessment-tools-ebook

Book 3. GDPR GAP Assessment by Process

https://bookboon.com/en/gdpr-gap-analysis-by-process-ebook

Data Protection (GDPR) Audit Guide – Five Parts (Five E-books)

Book 1. Data Protection Audit Process

https://bookboon.com/en/data-protection-audit-process-i-ebook

Book 2. DP Audit Questionnaires

https://bookboon.com/en/dp-audit-questionnaires-ii-ebook

Book 3. DP Audit Report

https://bookboon.com/en/dp-audit-report-ebook

Book 4. DP Audit Support Tools 1

https://bookboon.com/en/dp-audit-support-tools-1-ebook

Book 5. DP Audit Support Tools 2

https://bookboon.com/en/dp-audit-support-tools-2-ebook

The GDPR Employees' Guide – Six Parts (Six E-books)

Book 1. Effective Personal Data Practices: The GDPR Employees' Guide - Part I

https://bookboon.com/en/effective-personal-data-practices-ebook

Book 2. Managing Data Subject Rights: The GDPR Employees' Guide - Part II

https://bookboon.com/en/managing-data-subject-rights-ebook

Book 3. Managing Personal Data Breaches: The GDPR Employees' Guide - Part III

https://bookboon.com/en/managing-personal-data-breaches-ebook

Book 4. Assessing Information Risks: The GDPR Employees' Guide - Part IV

https://bookboon.com/en/assessing-information-risks-ebook

Book 5. Assessing Privacy Risks: The GDPR Employees' Guide - Part V

https://bookboon.com/en/assessing-privacy-risks-ebook

Book 6. Personal Data Support Tools: The GDPR Employees' Guide - Part VI

https://bookboon.com/en/personal-data-support-tools-ebook

Specialized Privacy Books

Book 1. The CEO's Guide to GDPR Compliance: The guide for C-Suite Members to ensure GDPR compliance, bookboon.com, 2017

https://bookboon.com/en/the-ceos-guide-to-gdpr-compliance-ebook

Book 2. GDPR and Travel Industry, bookboon.com, 2018

https://bookboon.com/en/gdpr-and-travel-industry-ebook

Book 3. Data Protection (GDPR) Guide

`https://bookboon.com/en/data-protection-gdpr-guide-ebook`

Book 4. Data Governance Controls, bookboon.com, 2019

`https://bookboon.com/en/data-governance-controls-ebook`

Privacy Books in Portuguese

Book 1. Sistema de gestão privacidade e proteção de dados:
Guia de Privacidade e Proteção de Dados – Vol I

`https://bookboon.com/pt/sistema-de-gestao-privacidade-e-protecao-de-dados-ebook`

Sistema de privacidade de dados

`https://bookboon.com/en/sistema-de-privacidade-de-dados-ebook`

Estratégias e planos de privacidade de dados

`https://bookboon.com/en/estrategias-e-planos-de-privacidade-de-dados-ebook`

Avaliação de Impacto de Proteção de Dados

`https://bookboon.com/en/avaliacao-de-impacto-de-protecao-de-dados-ebook`

Controles especializados de proteção de dados

`https://bookboon.com/en/controles-especializados-de-protecao-de-dados-ebook`

Questionários de auditoria de privacidade de dados

`https://bookboon.com/en/questionarios-de-auditoria-de-privacidade-de-dados-ebook`

Business Management Books

Corporate Performance

Book 1. How to improve your company's performance

http://bookboon.com/en/how-to-improve-your-companys-performance-ebook

Book 2. Improving Corporate Performance with BSC

http://bookboon.com/en/improving-performance-with-balanced-scorecard-ebook

Book 3. Auditing and Improving Business Performance

https://www.amazon.com/dp/B0088I8IVY

Book 4. Case Studies in Internal Controls

https://bookboon.com/en/case-studies-in-internal-controls-ebook

Book 5. How to Improve Your Production (Part 1)

http://bookboon.com/en/how-to-improve-your-production-part-i-ebook

Book 6. How to Improve Your Production (Part 2)

http://bookboon.com/en/how-to-improve-your-production-part-ii-ebook

SME – GDPR Books

Book 1. SME GDPR Guide

https://bookboon.com/en/sme-gdpr-guide-ebook

Book 2. SME GDPR Daily Operations Manual

https://bookboon.com/en/sme-gdpr-daily-operations-manual-ebook

Book 3. SME GDPR Support Tools

https://bookboon.com/en/sme-gdpr-support-tools-ebook

Managing SMEs

Book 1. Managing your SME more effectively (Part 1)

http://bookboon.com/en/managing-your-sme-more-effectively-part-i-ebook

Book 2. Managing your SME more effectively (Part 2)

http://bookboon.com/en/managing-your-sme-more-effectively-part-ii-ebook

SME Internal Controls

Book 1. SME Internal Controls Guide

https://bookboon.com/en/sme-internal-controls-guide-ebook

Book 2. SME Plans, Policies and Procedures: Book 2

https://bookboon.com/en/sme-plans-policies-and-procedures-2-ebook

Book 3. SME Auditing Toolkit - Book 3

https://bookboon.com/en/sme-auditing-toolkit-book-3-ebook

Human Aspects of Management Controls

Book 1. Achieving Better Implementation of Controls: The Human Aspects of Management Controls - Part I

http://bookboon.com/en/achieving-better-implementation-of-controls-ebook

Book 2. Tools Supporting Better Implementation of Controls: The Human Aspects of Management Controls - Part II

http://bookboon.com/en/tools-supporting-better-implementation-of-controls-ebook

Duty of Care

Books 1 to 8. "Duty of Care" small e-books, accessible at

http://bookboon.com/en/governance-aspects-of-duty-of-care-ebook

http://bookboon.com/en/operations-aspects-of-duty-of-care-ebook

http://bookboon.com/en/principles-and-methods-of-duty-of-care-ebook

http://bookboon.com/en/plans-of-duty-of-care-ebook

http://bookboon.com/en/policies-of-duty-of-care-ebook

http://bookboon.com/en/hr-management-controls-of-duty-of-care-ebook

http://bookboon.com/en/the-duty-of-care-management-approach-part-1-ebook

http://bookboon.com/en/implementing-duty-of-care-duties-part-2-ebook

Workplace Wellness

Book 1. Approaching Workplace Wellness

https://bookboon.com/en/approaching-workplace-wellness-ebook

Book 2. Workplace Wellness – Governance and Spirituality

https://bookboon.com/en/workplace-wellness-governance-and-spirituality-ebook

Book 3. Workplace Wellness: Relationships and Resilience

https://bookboon.com/en/workplace-wellness-relationships-and-resilience-ebook

Book 4. How to Improve Your Workplace Wellness: Volume II

https://bookboon.com/en/how-to-improve-your-workplace-wellness-volume-ii-ebook

Book 5. How to Improve Your Workplace Wellness: Volume III
https://bookboon.com/en/how-to-improve-your-workplace-wellness-volume-iii-ebook

Book 6. Corporate Wellness: Management and Evaluation Toolkit
http://bookboon.com/en/corporate-wellness-ebook

Virtual Management and Remote Working Books

Virtual Management

Book 1: Managing a Virtual Company - Book 1
https://bookboon.com/en/managing-a-virtual-company-ebook

Book 2: Internal Controls for Virtual Companies - Book 2
https://bookboon.com/en/internal-controls-for-virtual-companies-book-2-ebook

Book 3: Virtual Workplace Support Tools - Book 3
https://bookboon.com/en/virtual-workplace-support-tools-book-3-ebook

Book 4: Virtual Workplace HR Policies - Book 4
https://bookboon.com/en/virtual-workplace-hr-policies-book-4-ebook

Remote Working

Book 1. Corporate Practices to Establish Working Remotely
https://bookboon.com/en/corporate-practices-to-establish-working-remotely-ebook

Book 2. Remote Workers Handbook
https://bookboon.com/en/remote-workers-handbook-ebook

Book 3. Working from Home Auditing
https://bookboon.com/en/working-from-home-auditing-ebook
Book 4. Working from Home Toolkit
https://bookboon.com/en/working-from-home-toolkit-ebook

Personal Development
Personal Development

Book 1. How to Reduce Occupational Stress
http://bookboon.com/en/how-to-reduce-occupational-stress-ebook
Book 2. Seven Milestones for a Better Life
http://bookboon.com/en/seven-milestones-for-a-better-life-ebook
Book 3. Stress: Learning from the Ancient Greeks
https://bookboon.com/en/stress-learning-from-the-ancient-greeks-ebook
Book 4. Stress Management Support Tools
https://bookboon.com/en/stress-management-support-tools-ebook
Book 5. Live More Happily: The Ancient Greek Way
https://bookboon.com/en/live-more-happily-the-ancient-greek-way-ebook
Book 6. Corporate Happiness Improvement Tools
https://bookboon.com/en/corporate-happiness-improvement-tools-ebook
Book 7. Tools to Improve Your Personal Happiness
https://bookboon.com/en/tools-to-improve-your-personal-happiness-ebook

Ancient Greek Wisdom Books

Book 1. Pre-Classical Greek Wisdom for A Better Life
https://www.smashwords.com/books/view/701271

Book 2. The Pandora Way: Ancient Greek Wisdom for a better life
https://www.morebooks.de/store/gb/book/the-pandora-way:-ancient-greek-wisdom-for-a-better-life/isbn/978-3-659-53633-5

Book 3. Pre-Classical Greek Pearls of Wisdom
https://www.morebooks.shop/shop-ui/shop/product/9786205634042

Book 4: Pérolas Gregas de Sabedoria Pré-Clássica (Portuguese)
https://www.morebooks.de/shop-ui/shop/product/9786205737873

Book 5: Vorklassische griechische Perlen der Weisheit (German)
https://www.morebooks.de/shop-ui/shop/product/9786205737934

Book 6: Perlas de sabiduría de la Grecia preclásica (Spanish)
https://www.morebooks.de/shop-ui/shop/product/9786205737941

Book 7: Perles de sagesse de la Grèce préclassique (French)
https://www.morebooks.de/shop-ui/shop/product/9786205737965

Book 8: Perle di saggezza della Grecia preclassica (Italian)
https://www.morebooks.de/shop-ui/shop/product/9786205737972

Book 9: Доклассические греческие жемчужины мудрости (Russian)
https://www.morebooks.de/shop-ui/shop/product/9786205737989

Article: "The Odyssey Story: Moral Lessons for today's Leaders and Managers," published in "The IIC Internal Controls e-Magazine," Vol.4, Issue 2, August 2023, pg. 20-35
https://online.fliphtml5.com/prsun/oetx/

Management Tools

Tool 1. Data Protection Impact Assessment (EU GDPR Requirement)
https://flevy.com/browse/business-document/data-protection-impact-assessment-eu-gdpr-requirement-2543

Tool 2. EU GDPR Quick Readiness Action Plan

http://flevy.com/browse/business-document/eu-gdpr-quick-readiness-action-plan-2896

Tool 3. GDPR Personal Data Inventory Register

https://flevy.com/browse/business-document/gdpr-personal-data-inventory-register-3415

Tool 4. GDPR Audit Tool #01_Data Confidentiality Assessment

https://flevy.com/browse/business-document/gdpr-audit-tool-01data-confidentiality-assessment-3419

Tool 5. GDPR Audit Tool #02_HR Cultural Controls Assessment

https://flevy.com/browse/business-document/gdpr-audit-tool02hr-cultural-controls-assessment-3420

Tool 6. GDPR Audit Tool#03_Data Privacy Principles Compliance Assessment

https://flevy.com/browse/business-document/gdpr-audit-tool03data-privacy-principles-assessment-3421

Tool 7. How to Implement Corporate Policies Better

https://flevy.com/browse/business-document/how-to-implement-corporate-policies-better-1668

Tool 8. Audit Report Model and Sample

https://flevy.com/browse/business-document/audit-report-model-and-sample-268

Tool 9. Auditing and Improving Business Performance

https://flevy.com/browse/business-document/auditing-and-improving-business-performance-216

Tool 10. ISO 27001/27002 (2022) - Security Audit Questionnaires (Tool 1).

https://flevy.com/browse/marketplace/iso-27001-27002-2022--security-audit-questionnaires-tool-1-7408

ISO 27001: 2022 Compliance Support Tools

Tool 1. ISO 27K Compliance Support Toolkit – Book 1

This book (**ISO 27K Compliance Support Toolkit – Bool 1**) includes several (91) recommended security compliance measures, such as over *28 plans, over 12 policies, over 27 procedures, and over 18 other support tools.* These are designed to support you in implementing better the 37 ISO 27K controls and their requirements outlined in ISO 27001:2022, Annex A5, Organizational Controls.

Available at

https://flevy.com/browse/marketplace/iso-27k-compliance-support-toolkit--book-1-7999

Tool 2. ISO 27K Compliance Support Toolkit – Book 2

This book (**ISO 27K Compliance Support Toolkit – Book 2**) includes several (46) recommended security compliance measures (RCMs), such as over 21 *plans, over 15 policies, over 12 procedures, and 4 other support tools.* These are designed to support you in implementing better the 22 ISO 27K controls and their requirements outlined in ISO 27001:2022, Annex A6 (People Controls) and A7 (Physical Controls).

Available at

https://flevy.com/browse/marketplace/iso-27k-compliance-support-toolkit--book-2-8001

Tool 3. ISO 27K Compliance Support Toolkit – Book 3

This book (**ISO 27K Compliance Support Toolkit - Book 3**) includes 79 recommended security compliance measures (RCM), such as 21 *plans, 26 policies, 8 procedures, and 24 other support tools.* These are designed to support you in implementing better the 34 ISO 27K controls and their requirements outlined in ISO 27001:2022, Annex A8 (Technological (Tech) Controls).

Available at

https://flevy.com/browse/marketplace/iso-27k-compliance-support-toolkit--book-3-8002

Tool 4. ISO 27K Compliance Support Toolkit - Book 4

This book (**ISO 27K Compliance Support Toolkit – Book 4**) includes an example of a statement of applicability and an example of a gap assessment. These are designed to support you in implementing better the 93 ISO 27K controls and their requirements outlined in ISO 27001:2022, Annex A.

Available at

```
https://flevy.com/browse/marketplace/iso-27k-
compliance?support-toolkit--book-4-8003
```

Tool 5. ISO 27K 2022 Version – Security Audit Questionnaires

This tool (set of spreadsheets) contains five parts with 800 questions and an evaluation method, for all control issues and areas (over 93) of the ISO 27K 2022 version on all aspects of information security, as defined in this ISO standard. These questionnaires may be used to support your efforts in assessing whether your company, organization, or business function or department (herein "company") complies with the requirements of ISO security standard ISO 27001/27002: 2022 version.

Available at

```
https://flevy.com/browse/marketplace/iso-27001-27002-2022--
security-audit-questionnaires-tool-1-7408
```

M11. ISO 27001/27002 Security Audit Questionnaire

```
https://flevy.com/browse/business-document/iso-27001-27002-
security-audit-questionnaire-2622
```

M12. ISO 27001 ISMS: Statement of Applicability

```
https://flevy.com/browse/business-document/iso-27001-isms-
statement-of-applicability-1666
```

Tool 13. Teleworking Audit Toolkit

```
https://flevy.com/browse/business-document/teleworking-
audit-toolkit-5103
```

Tool 14. GDPR and LGPD Compliance: Implementation Guidance

```
https://flevy.com/browse/marketplace/gdpr-and-lgpd-
compliance-5942
```

Tool 15. LGPD Quick Implementation Action Plan

https://flevy.com/browse/marketplace/lgpd-quick-implementation-action-plan-5976

Tool 16. LGPD Processing Records Tool

https://flevy.com/browse/marketplace/lgpd-processing-records-tool-5983

Tool 17. A Manager's Duty of Care Audit Toolkit

http://flevy.com/browse/business-document/a-managers-duty-of-care-audit-toolkit-2977

Disclaimer

The material, concepts, ideas, plans, policies, procedures, forms, methods, tools, etc., presented, described, and analyzed in all chapters and appendices, are for educational and training purposes only. These may be used only, possibly, as an indicative base set and should be customized by each organization, after careful and considerable thought as to the needs and requirements of each organization, taking into effect the implications and aspects of the legal, national, religious, philosophical, cultural and social environments, and expectations, within which each organization operates and exists.

Every possible effort has been made to ensure that the information contained in this book is accurate at the time of going to press, and the publishers and the author cannot accept responsibility for any errors or omissions, however caused. No responsibility for loss or damage occasioned to any person acting, or refraining from action, as a result of the material in this publication can be accepted by the publisher or the author.

Index

A

Access point, 44, 61, 62
Advanced persistent threat, 2, 3, 12
Algorithm, 105
Analyzing log files, 52
Annual training program, 96
Antivirus program, 105
Application software, 105, 107
Attempted access, 2–4, 41, 43
Avoidance tactics, 44

B

Backup, 33, 45, 73, 88, 106
BSR, *see* Board Security
        Responsibilities (BSR)
Board Security Responsibilities
        (BSR), 28, 29

C

CEO, *see* Chief executive
        officer (CEO)
Chief executive officer (CEO), 93
Cloud computing, 106
Company and regulatory
        authorities, 46

Computer virus, 106
Consent, 19, 24
Continuing professional
        education (CPE), 109, 112
Controllers, 7, 9–11, 13, 19, 20, 22,
        25, 55–57, 63, 71, 93, 94
Cookies, 106
Corporate performance, 138
Corporate security measures, 16
Cost comparison, 44
CPE, *see* Continuing professional
        education (CPE)
Critical information
        security terms
    advanced persistent
        threat, 3
    attempted access, 4
    DoS attack, 4
    malware, 3
    phishing, 3
    ransomware, 4
    unauthorized access, 4
Cross-functional Personal Data
        Breach Incident Response
        Group, 34
Cybercrime, 49–53, 129
Cybercrime investigators, 49, 50

© The Editor(s) (if applicable) and The Author(s),
under exclusive license to APress Media, LLC, part of Springer Nature 2024
J. Kyriazoglou, *Information Security Incident and Data Breach Management*,
https://doi.org/10.1007/979-8-8688-0870-8

GPSR Compliance
The European Union's (EU) General Product Safety Regulation (GPSR) is a set
of rules that requires consumer products to be safe and our obligations to
ensure this.

If you have any concerns about our products, you can contact us on

ProductSafety@springernature.com

In case Publisher is established outside the EU, the EU authorized
representative is:

Springer Nature Customer Service Center GmbH
Europaplatz 3
69115 Heidelberg, Germany